SO-BJI-873

UNROMANTIC SPAIN

THE ESCORIAL

UNROMANTIC SPAIN

BY
MARIO PRAZ

ALFRED A. KNOPF

NEW YORK AND LONDON

FIRST PUBLISHED IN 1929

SET IN MONOTYPE PASTONCHI AND
PRINTED IN GREAT BRITAIN FOR
ALFRED A. KNOPF, INC., BY HAZELL,
WATSON AND VINEY, LTD., LONDON
AND AYLESBURY

*This book appeared originally in Italian with the
title " Penisola Pentagonale" (Milan, Alpes
publ., 1928), and has been revised and translated
into English by the author, who is under obliga‹
tion for criticism and advice to his friends Major
Orlo Williams, Professor Allen Mawer, and
Professor W. E. Collinson.*

TO

ORLO WILLIAMS

TO WHOSE SUGGESTION
THIS ENGLISH VERSION IS DUE

ILLUSTRATIONS

7

INTRODUCTION

Il y a des choses que tout le monde dit parce
qu'elles ont été dites une fois—MONTESQUIEU

IF I were to tell you that I saw in Biscay ladies carrying under their arms little sucking-pigs adorned
with collars of many-coloured ribbons, that in
Madrid I saw the King come out on the balcony of
his palace in order to satisfy the legitimate curiosity
of a deputation of women with child, and stay there
until they were cured of the desire to devour him
with their eyes, that in Seville, during the Holy
Week processions, I watched the flagellants earning
the gratitude of the ladies by sprinkling their clothes
with spurts of blood, and in Barcelona, during a bull-
fight, the bull climbing the steps of the amphi-
theatre, and the spectators, scared by the mountain-
eering propensities of the two-horned climber,
swarming down into the arena; finally, that everywhere I saw persons of quality displaying, from their
earliest childhood, tortoise-shell spectacles of a size
proportional to their rank and state, and *iettatori*
obliged to blindfold their supposed evil eye,—if I told

11

you these and similar Iberian amenities, you might think me very picturesque, but as for believing me, I dare say you would give me little credit. If, however, I pictured to you "old Spanish towns languorous beneath the warm sun and the scent of orange blos/ soms, castellated mansions and Moorish arabesques, a proud people hugging fierce passions beneath their cloaks, guitars and castanets, donkeys and courteous peasants, long white roads and snowy ribbed sierras, quaint old market/squares, narrow streets with balconies atop and animated *paseos*, gar/ dens everywhere, swimming in the sun," then I sur/ mise that, without ceasing to think me very pic/ turesque, you would take my words in real earnest. Because, in this latter case, I should only be enumer/ ating the component parts which go to make up the fascination, colour and romance of Spain, according to the traditional formula worked out by the Ger/ man and French Romantics, perfected by Théophile Gautier, and consecrated in the lyric prose of Thos. Cook & Son, Ltd., which I have just reproduced in its rhetorical purity.

However, when Gautier was preaching the gospel of picturesque Spain, and giving the finishing touch to the picture in which Mérimée, Musset, Hugo, had collaborated, when he was making of Granada the Mecca of Romanticism, he knew very well, the sportive Parisian tourist, that he was faking a man/

nered Spain. See how mischievously he winks: *"Nous étions enchantés. Le pittoresque demandé se produisait en abondance."* Therefore, indulging in his partiality for colour, he dishes up people, land‹ scapes, monuments, with picturesque condiment, in the same way as the *chef* at Poccardi's, in order not to shatter the illusions of the English and Americans visiting Paris, floods every Italian dish with a deluge of tomato sauce. An Italian dish without tomato sauce would be like a water‹colour of the Roman Campagna without a blood‹red sunset. The guest of the Poccardi Restaurant is entitled to the tomato sauce, and the traveller to Spain has a claim to the picturesque. As a matter of fact, Gautier was so en‹ grossed in his painting, that one can hardly doubt he eventually came to believe in it himself. *Fumisterie*, mystification, plays funny tricks on one, sometimes! I have derived no little amusement from counting how many times the adjective *pittoresque* occurs in the *Voyage en Espagne*. I had first contemplated tabulating here the results of my quaint research, but since I have heard of an American scholar who is just working at a thesis, complete with statistics, on that important subject, I realise that he has a prior claim to the field, and I forbear from forestalling here his scientific demonstration.

Unfortunately, his readers took long‹haired, monocled Théo very seriously. And, without listen‹

ing to the *doléances pittoresques* of the humorous author, who, between the lines, lets one guess how that voyage of his was little else than a merry masquerade he had undertaken in order to weather that *prosaïque et malencontreux* year 1840—which, by the way, seems so picturesque to us—,generations of superficial readers have sworn by the *Voyage en Espagne*, and indelibly stereotyped the formula. Even now whoever goes to Spain for pleasure expects to see a romantic country, with dark señoras spending the whole of their lives on the balcony, national dances clattering with castanets and clamorous with *¡ole!*, beggars draped in their rags like emperors— *sublimité du haillon,*—with brigands and mystics and stern-looking hidalgos, Don Quixote, Gines de Pasamonte, Lazarillo de Tormes, Gil Blas, Saint Teresa, Carmen, Conchita, and, in short, *du sang, de la volupté, de la mort.* The movies pander to the public taste with sensational stories whose tenor is generally to this effect:

THE RIGHT OF THE STRONG

A Night of Love

"A romance of pure, true love from man to man, which is eternal and of all times. The raptures and sufferings, the despair and bliss of love, the whole story of the warm, throbbing human heart, with its

SPANISH TRAVEL A CENTURY AGO

needs and its glory, is here lived through in one single, fast-fleeting night.

"A TALE OF ANCIENT SPAIN, with its chivalric grace, its lightly inflammable passion, its fascinating women, and its deep Moorish nights."

"I long to see a really wicked Carmen"—declared to me an enthusiastic English lady, who had got fixed in her head a famous repartee from Mérimée's immortal story (—*Tu es le diable, lui disais-je.* —*Oui, me répondit-elle.* Simple and fatal, eh?). With the prospect of such an exciting experience, the good lady paid fifty guineas to Mr. Thos. Cook, who showed her the first-class hotels of Spain, which, needless to say, are exactly like the first-class hotels all over the world. The same lady never failed to throw up her hands in admiration for the charming Spanish mystics—she had never read them—and found that even Velázquez was picturesque, just as if he had been a Fortuny of a sort.

A most efficient bank clerk in the City, while lunching with me at Pym's, confessed that his secret aspiration was to do Spain on the back of a mule. One reached the Spanish frontier, hired a mule, and proceeded to the heart of the romantic country, looking just like one of *them*. That was the idea. He had got it from a book. Bank clerks and well-to-do ladies have some curious imaginings: the more humdrum their ordinary life, the more unbridled is the course of their fancy.

"Don't you really believe in picturesque Spain?" I hear somebody asking. "Are you by any chance a partisan of the Europeanisation of Spain?" I believe there is still something to be gleaned in Spain, by people yearning for picturesqueness. They ought, however, to start by giving up the idea of finding it where it is advertised. Tourists going to Spain with a smattering of preconceived notions derived from any current romantic concoction, invariably come back disappointed. They dreamt of finding another Italy (the only country which never has, and never will, disappoint travellers), and they find something quite different, for which they have no cue. They find the country squalid, because they were not pre-pared to find it monotonous; they find the buildings not half as impressive as they had anticipated from the pictures, because they threw round those pic-tures the glamour of well-known Italian scenes. And as for the Spanish character, they are bound to be disappointed if they have taken literally the tag about the "proud people hugging fierce passions beneath their cloaks." The Spaniards are, as a rule, matter-of-fact, and infinitely less romantic than Eng-lish spinsters and holiday-bound bank clerks. But, somehow, all that world of passions and habits dis-covered among the Italians by the first hunters after the exotic, the Elizabethans, and rediscovered by Stendhal and the Romantics, has been harnessed also on the back of the Spanish nation, as a consequence of a hasty generalisation about the South. Because in both countries there were banditti and lazzaroni, and people were jealous and killed for love's sake, it was assumed that the features of the Italian and Spanish characters fundamentally coincided. There has happened, in this respect, something not very different from what one sees in certain Italian landscapes painted by Danish and German artists at the beginning of last century. No matter which part of Italy those artists are painting, be it Genoa or Florence or whatnot, they invariably people the foreground with figures dressed in the costume of the *ciociari*, i.e. the peasants of the Roman Campagna. But there is a better instance, in which we actually seem to get at the root of the misunderstanding. In Kyd's *Spanish Tragedy* there is nothing Spanish apart from the title and the names of three or four among the characters. The words used by the wouldbe Spaniards to give the exotic thrill to the Elizabethan audience are Italian words, and the action is Senecan tragedy as interpreted in the light of Italian Renaissance manners.

For all this, I maintain that the Spanish national character can be a source of the picturesque for foreigners, chiefly by way of contrast. The English man (I do not speak here of the Cook-driven tourist, who travels about, so to say, shut up in a trunk) who has opportunity of staying in Spain for some time, and somehow manages to talk the language, cannot but find the first contact with Spanish people rather refreshing. Why, here are human beings who are not mere automatons with ready-made feelings and hopelessly civilised habits. They are alive, they have extremely engaging manners. An Englishman will feel the contrast the more striking if the only foreign country he has visited so far is Northern France, where a cynical matter-of-factness predomi-nates. Spaniards do not grudge you the display of their quaint souls, as the hard, disappointing French do. Spaniards have plenty of time to loaf around you like curious pets, while you sit comfortably at the table of a café, and watch and find amusement. The truth is that Spaniards seem to do for the whole of their time what an Englishman longs to do all the week, and is able to achieve only in the few hours of the sleepy, stodgy Sunday: Spaniards are constantly found guilty of that darling sin, idleness. And, mark you, it is not idleness in a dull suburban garden, beneath a grey sky, or in a stuffy sitting-room, while it is drizzling outside. Their idleness gloriously basks in the sun. Curiously enough, idleness is an English more than a Spanish ideal, but Englishmen cannot help being at work, just as Spaniards cannot

help being idle. In either case, a type of civilisation
is carried on, irrespective of individual tendencies.
Everything seems to smooth down so easily, in the
human affable Spanish atmosphere. One feels that,
even if a bill were to fall due to-morrow, and one
had no money, everything would be made smooth
and nice in quite a friendly way. After you have
lived in Spain for some time, everybody seems
to be your friend; you are called by your Christian
name, you are patted on the shoulder just that
little touch that causes you to feel at home and
patronised—a perfectly delightful country to live
in, if life were to be, as, alas, it is not, a protracted
week-end.

This is the charm of Spain: an engaging spontan-
eity of manners, and friendliness. Or, at least, so one
thinks at first, until one is shocked by the discovery
that friendly words mean little more than nothing,
little more than the "thank you" your servant says
on being sent on some errand, or the "sorry" the
person sitting next to you at the table says when you
trouble him for the cruet.

"*Per comodidad de sus amigos patrón*"—reads the
casticísima inscription over the gate of a house. That
inscription might as well be changed into the
Dantesque "*Lasciate ogni speranza, voi ch'entrate.*"
For, if you expect the master of the house to welcome
you and give you food and lodging, you are grossly

mistaken. That happened, perhaps, in the times in which the Spaniards were still influenced by Arab civilisation, when a private house was the only inn and shelter available for a wretched traveller. The formula still persists to-day, side by side with such other amusing relics as *"póngame usted a los pies de su señora,"* but a Spaniard would no more dream of flinging his door open to welcome you, than you of falling on your knees before his wife. Those formu-las are hollow; their substance is as dead as the dodo. But Spaniards stick to them, just in the same way as they continue to idle about their sunny *plazas* as they did three thousand years ago; they stick to them because they feel no desire to do away with them. They leave them about partly because it does not cross their minds that they could easily dispense with them, partly because those formulas add a cer-tain decorum and glamour to social relations, with-out committing one to anything. They leave them about as they would leave rubbish about the streets or as they would let tottering walls totter for ever, so far as they were concerned.

A very picturesque experience can be suggested to a romantic Englishman. Let him reply in the affirmative to the Spanish friend who, on the point of parting from him at the door of his own house, asks him: *"¿Quiere usted comer conmigo?"* (Would you like to have a meal with me?) Let him say:

"*Quiero.*" Or let him praise the umbrella of the Spaniard who has sheltered him from a sudden shower. "*Es de usted,*" the Spaniard is sure to reply. Let then the Englishman accept the offer and try to obtain the wonderful umbrella. Let him just try and see——

As for Spanish friendliness, it certainly *does* help to make life agreeable, provided you do not try to scrape off its veneer. I do not imply that Spaniards are false. They are not. It is understood that you must help to keep up the show of universal friendliness, just as it is understood in England that certain subjects are deliberately excluded from polite conversation. Still, the subject *is* there, the road *is* there even when you place in it the notice "No road." In the same way every Spaniard knows that, in spite of all outward demonstrations, real friendliness is *not* there; and when a thing is an open secret, nobody can be taken in and complain of duplicity. What you find when you scrape off the veneer of Spanish engaging manners is the desire to get you to play into their hand, to wink at something or other, to be one of them. It is part of the game. No truer representation of Spanish life has ever been given than in Benavente's *Intereses creados.* Life is a net of organised interests: you must not do anything to disturb it. You may have very strong reasons for objecting to somebody's actions, but that somebody is your friend's friend, therefore you are expected to wink. The ultimate aim of the system is to make life infinitely easier by underhand ways. Instead of facing difficulties, you get round them with the help of an influential friend. In this way, true, some of the noblest things of life are stultified, but, on the other hand, you can push on with the least personal effort: the ideal of an indolent people.

There is an ugly Italian word for this kind of practice. It is *camorra*. But Spaniards will feel shocked if you try to use that word in connection with their society. Because that kind of practice is so much the rule there, that it is the reverse course which is liable to be found shocking, as being against the established code of morals. The chief aim of the Spanish Dictatorship has been to put an end to that traditional basis of national life, and to turn a new leaf, a European leaf. How far Primo de Rivera has succeeded in it, I will not be so rash as to judge; but up to the present one feels rather inclined to repeat the French proverb: *Plus ça change, plus c'est la même chose.*

But the guileless tourist need not be initiated into the open secrets of Spanish life. He will take delight in the marionettes and ignore the wires. He does not aim at establishing business relations with the people; all he asks from them is that they should not spoil the show by a too obtrusive display of the less

pleasing sides of their lives. His appreciation of the
natives is not based on utilitarian considerations, but
on æsthetic principles. He knows that the time of
his departure is near at hand, and he forbears from
asking admission to the intimacy of local society.
He is a dumb witness. Like the chorus of the Greek
tragedy, he can do nothing to alter the destinies of
those who are round him. There is nothing he can
say to them. As if the faces, gestures, actions he sees
were really brought to him by the light of a distant
planet which had started a thousand years ago. The
life he sees displayed under his eyes might as well
belong to history, since the space in which the
traveller moves is endowed with a different speed
from the space of those who abide in the country;
and not to belong to the same space is equivalent to
not being contemporary. The very fact of being a
passing stranger is enough to give to the circum-
stances that character of things for ever completed
which they inevitably possess when they belong to
the past.

For me, for instance, a journey is like a *memento
mori*. The imminence of the departure, the surmise
that my first visit to a new town will be also my last,
gives a stamp of finality to my impressions. To de-
part is a sort of dying: the Italian sonneteers of
the sixteenth century said it before the French
novelists: *partir c'est mourir un peu.* Every new town,

while she welcomes me, puts her hand to her lips
bidding adieu. So that in any new town I visit for a
short while I feel myself already vanished, like a
ghost; I am there, and yet I am absent, a wraith of
my everyday self, a dumb witness.

What difference is there for me between wander-
ing through the deserted streets of dead Pompeii or
the animated streets of half-alive Cordoba? In both
cases I am alien. The inhabitants of Pompeii are far
away from me in material time, but those of the
Omayyad town whom I see with a traveller's eye are
far away from me in a spiritual time. And what
difference is there between breathing the life of my
own fantasy into the deserted streets and forums,
and watching in front of me men of flesh and blood
whom the imminent hour will take away from me
for ever? Is the Lozana Andaluza less alive for me
than the woman I saw kneeling before the Crucifix
of the Plazuela de los Dolores, hiding in her hands
her face which I was pleased to imagine beautiful?
For a moment I am in the soul of the imaginary
woman as in that of the woman who is in my presence; for it is but an illusion to think that, if I wanted
to, I might approach the latter while I never might
approach the former. I know that I shall not approach the kneeling woman, that I am not going to
talk to her: she by no means differs from the other
who is only a picture of my imagination. In a sense

24

Photo : L. Elton

CASTILLA LA VIEJA

Waste Land seen from Coca Castle

CORDOBA

Plazuela de los Dolores

24]

she is dead to me as I am dead to her; she is life as it is saluted and felt by somebody who is dying, by a traveller about to leave. She is an image. Although my footsteps echo on the grass-grown cobble-stones, although those lamps perched on the top of wrought iron branches actually burn round the Crucifix, although I can touch those walls and feel the close air of the clouded night, everything is but an image. Between me and the praying woman everything is said, for nothing is said. Does she feel my presence in the little square as silent as a church-yard? She has heard my footsteps echoing through the tortuous streets, drawing near, being reverberated by the very walls of the little square, stopping, but she does not turn round. I am just *somebody* for her. For me, she is *somebody*. Two people who ignore each other, who only once in their lives, while performing the allotted itineraries, pass each other, to be, the next moment, far away for ever. And what difference does it make if our courses skirt each other at the distance of a second, or at the distance of a century?

To travel is to feel death creeping in every minute; therefore, to travel is also to feel life as a crisp experience, as an adventure which is sure not to be repeated again. Romance does not so much belong to the new countries one visits, as to the very fact of travelling in itself. I seem never to come across so many faces and acts deserving attention, as when I am travelling. To travel is to grow young again; our soul becomes again sensitive to impressions, like wax. While I am travelling I take interest in people with whom, in ordinary life, I would by no means be eager to make the acquaintance. Is the everyday-man wrong in casting an indifferent, aloof glance at the faces he sees—well-knowing that the apparent differences cannot make up for the boredom, the trivial monotony common to all and sundry—or is the traveller wrong when, faced with a new human being, he proclaims: "Nobody, nobody is like him"?

How many times must I have travelled in Italy in the same compartment with strolling players, without ever bestowing on them so much as a glance! But in that train to Salamanca, with low windows and a cumbersome bulging stove, the two strolling players appeared to me as eternal types. Why, after all, should I imagine that they were actors? She had her cheeks and lips carefully rouged like a Parisian; she was young, and could be taken for a *cocotte*. As for him, a touch of bohemianism in the hair, of excessive mobility in the face, of gaudiness in the dress and shoes, betrayed a non-virile profession—perhaps a dancer, or a singer, or a player—or, who knows? a hairdresser, *coiffeur pour dames, Monsieur Charles*. Their bags were showy, but worn out; like

their clothes, they revealed a smartness of line, not
withstanding their lost spruceness. They were no
lovers; they were, apparently, husband and wife.
Still, at times, one might have thought they were
lovers. They had something curiously similar in
their appearances, like love-birds. I did not catch
what they said to each other in the hotel coach which
rattled us through dark streets. She looked nervous,
he looked worried. The light of a lamp caught her
eyes—the eyes of a frightened child, fixedly looking
at nothing, exiles in the midst of the surrounding
bistre. Just before reaching the hotel she passed a
lip-stick over her lips and powdered her nose. He
arranged his tie and the coloured silk handkerchief
in the pocket of his coat. Once in the office of the
hotel I laughed at my gloomy hypotheses. She had
put on the most engaging of smiles for the surly pro-
prietor, and clapped her hands like a child when she
learned the number of the room: "Sixteen! The
same as the other time, Claudio!" What hours of
happiness were promised by that apparently familiar
figure? They seemed to know the whole staff of the
hotel well; they were very liberal with their smiles.
Still that stagey glance of a fatal woman she cast on
the young awkward waiter who helped them in the
dining-room—was it not beyond the limits of
decency? But, no doubt, she produced it only in
order to get better helpings, *claro*: oh, she was a

minx! And the gawky *muchacho*, dazzled by that glance which for him stood for all the romance of life, transferred as gallantly as he could the stew and peas into the plate of the star—and, while doing so, he fumbled a little with his fingers.

Next day, I had forgotten them. That spring sky, all a web of little silver clouds and clear islets of blue, which enhanced the tawny and golden tones of the buildings, had transported me to a superhuman region, where only eternal stones and vast spaces were alive. I entered the courts decorated with cir⸱cumflex arches as I would have entered sleepy fairy palaces: Casa de las Conchas, Casa de la Salina, Irish College, Convento de las Dueñas with capitals like those of Persepolis in their symmetrical busts of animals kneeling back to back—I seemed to see nothing else but the honey⸱coloured stones of Dorada Salamanca against the silver April sky. Or, in the deserted cathedral, the procession of canons with long trailing cassocks, kneeling in front of the dean who waved the black banner with the red cross, so many times—as the standard⸱bearers do during the Palio at Siena. And about the cathedral, also, there hovered an air as of an abandoned fairy palace, of a vanished worship; and about the University, too, where the crimson velvet of the chairs had worn off under the dust of centuries of decay. Here Luís de León once spoke; here, until yesterday, spoke

Miguel de Unamuno. Do the letters engraved in the benches perpetuate their messages? No, the students of Luís de León, like the students of Unamuno, have only carved their own names and the usual idiotic or obscene arabesques. For whom did the priest wave his banner? For whom had the professor of the sixteenth and that of the nineteenth centuries spoken?

Everywhere neglect, oblivion, death! Only the stones and the sky were alive, the former motionless for ever, the latter always changing. But late at night, while I was roaming through the solitary uphill streets of the musty old town, at a turning (was it near the Seminario Conciliar?) my attention was caught by two figures which were moving in the dusk. They were walking apart, she close to the wall, swift, rigid, silent, he in the middle of the street, engaged in a long conciliatory argument. Their silhouettes seemed not unfamiliar to me. Her voice, though altered with anger, did not sound new: "*¡Me voy a Francia!*"—she broke out. They were the two strolling players. "*¡Me voy a Francia!*" —she kept repeating: it seemed impossible to draw other words out of the angry woman, who was skirting the walls, swiftly, as if driven by the violence of a final decision.

Next morning, at breakfast, I sought them in the *comedor*. They were not there. I set out again sight-seeing. But Salamanca was no longer for me the musty old town, the forsaken fairy place. What were the bygone ages of faith and science? What the vainly waved banners, the worn-off velvet of the chairs, the lofty spires, the distant silver vault of the sky? The two strolling players had crept in, and made of all Salamanca the stage of their diminutive tragedy.

How romantic is the traveller's fantasy! Perhaps, if the two strolling players had told me their story from beginning to end, I should have been bored to death: sure enough, a new very old story of common miseries and trivial grievances. Perhaps, after all, they were no strolling players either, and the cause of the quarrel may have been the refusal of a new frock, of a gewgaw, or maybe they were simply dis-appointed at not having won in that week's lottery.

Of this sort of picturesque the new traveller will find abundant store in the Spanish life he happens to observe from the outside. The less he knows Spaniards, the more will he find their ways novel, their faces interesting, their actions puzzling. Men are much more difficult to fathom than landscapes or buildings; and the traveller's ideal of the Spanish character may rest undisturbed, if he only takes the precaution of not learning the language and giving free rein to his imagination. But, alas, buildings and landscapes, and whatever is the written, carved, painted work of man, speak a universal language, and the traveller setting out with a mind furnished with ideal scenes will be long in finding them. He cannot help keeping his eyes open; and if his eyes have been prepared to receive a quick succession of romantic impressions, to witness that "flicker" of effects which is the very essence of the picturesque, then he had better read again his Gautier at home, instead of travelling to the land of his heart's desire. For, if there is a country in Europe where that essential quality of picturesqueness is least present, that country is Spain.

MARIO PRAZ.

Liverpool, November 1928.

UNROMANTIC SPAIN

C

Nihil novum, nihil varium, nihil, quod non
semel spectare sufficiat—*Plini Epiſt.* ix, 6

WHILE the legend of picturesque Spain is becoming
cheaper and cheaper, and the formula firſt put into
circulation by Gautier gets finally worn out in
Cook's prospectuses, nowadays whoever travels in
Spain is not long in noticing how the essence of that
country lies in the very antithesis of picturesqueness,
namely in a grandiose, overwhelming monotony.

Let those who can recall the impression received
upon firſt looking at the Italian rooms, and what
they felt on entering the Spanish ones, in the
National Gallery. In the former a feaſt of brilliant
colours, like a ſtreaming of oriflammes againſt the
sparkling emerald of the lagoons, all the colours of
the rainbow squeezed to the utmoſt of their essence;
airiness of clean-swept skies, serenity of deeply ex-
pressive faces, opulence of fine clothes, juicy fruits,
magnificent flowers. Such is the general impression,
and a closer inspection yields further delight: the
whole scale of colour and sentiment, with infinite
shades, seems to be enshrined in the bright canvases.
But whereas the colour of the sky dominates in the

Italian rooms, that of the earth rules in the Spanish section. One would almost infer that the Italian painters had got their education by stedfast gazing upon the spacious blue, and that the Spaniards, on the contrary, dazzled by the glare of the sun, had kept their eyes fixed on the brown earth, on the ochre and umber of their barren plateaux. With the Italian painters, grace takes the soft hues of the crystal horizon, *"dolce color d'oriental zaffiro,"* with the Spanish the soothing tints of soaked earth. Apart from the sulphureous gleam of El Greco's can‑ vases, the rest of the Spanish rooms seems to strike a single note, a brown note of cork and pumice‑stone, earthy. If two rooms are deemed insufficient for characterising the school of painting of a whole nation, think, if you can, of the Louvre, the Prado, the Seville and Valencia galleries; you must own then that, infinite as the variations may be, the funda‑ mental theme remains the same. There is Francisco Ribalta who takes after the earthiest among the Italian painters, the leaden, opaque Sebastiano del Piombo; there are the arid, cork‑like nudes of Ribera, in landscapes of rock and barren soil, soothed by a distant glimpse of the sky or by a gold gleam of sunset; there is the jaundiced conclave of bilious monks round the livid San Basilio, by Fran‑ cisco Herrera; there are the wooden virgins and saints of Zurbarán, as dull and stiff as a Queen of

Spades against the monotony of a brown back‹
ground; you have the tender auburn and grey hues
of Murillo's canvases with which to delight your eyes
just as you would delight your palate by crushing
against it *fondants* and sugared chestnuts (Murillo,
the great master of chocolate‹box painters!); you
see the unique Velázquez distil into matchless har‹
monies the whole earthy spirit of Spanish colour and
the stark crudity of the plateau atmosphere; you
find Goya as great in his dusky manner as he is in‹
different in the gay cartoons of the tapestries and in
the dummy‹like nude of the Maja; and, to use a
modern instance, you watch the contemporary
Zuloaga deriving muddy rivulets from the firm
sods of great Velázquez. No wonder the funda‹
mental tone of Spanish painting is "of the earth
earthy," a monotonous, powerful earthiness. It is
surely true that the surrounding world has a decisive
influence in the education of the eye.[1]

Whoever has travelled through Spain knows how
indelibly one is impressed by the aspect of the bare,
almost waste land, spread like a dry hide on the
salient ribs of the mountain ranges, which softens
into a supple tawny leather under the golden

[1] Even a foreigner like El Greco could not resist that influence.
A comparison has been suggested (by Mrs. Trapier in her book
on *El Greco*, 1925) between his *Prayer in the Garden*, with a jagged
rock towering in the centre, and Mantegna's treatment of the
same subject, with its dazzling blue sky.

caress of sunset. The satirical description of Fulvio Savojano, of the beginning of the seventeenth century, does not need much alteration to ring true also to-day:

"The kingdoms of Spain are some barren and waste, like Aragon and Galicia, some dreary and alpine, like Castille and Biscay, some mountainous and stony, like Catalonia and Navarre, some with few towns, like Valencia and Granada, some with a single one, like Cordoba and Jaen: fine fields of red sand which produce nothing but rosemary and wild lavender, fine plains where one comes across no more than one inhabited place in one day's journey, fine mountains of bare and broken stones, fine hills where there is no blade of grass, no drop of water, fine shelters of cabins, caverns and stables, fine towns all built of wood and mud."

From Sahagún, in the North, where one descries the aerial sky-line of the Cantabric Mountains (before long the landscape will become wooded and alpine) to the Puerto de Despeñaperros, in the South, at the gate of the Andalusian garden, there is no interruption in the monotonous expanse of desolate dusty lands, *dehesas y despoblados "sin materia de sensitiva recreación,"* where, in the spring, the rare brooks of a pure blue, the blue of gentians blossoming on crags, cause no less astonishment than the unsuspected tenderness of austere people.

The Castilian landscape offers in a raw state the alphabet of the Spanish painters; the few dominant colours of their palette are all displayed there. The Mancha beneath a lowering sky: in the foreground stripes of reddish and malachite-green soil, then terraces and terraces, as far as eye can reach, the farthermost occupying the sky-line with its dismal limestone paleness veined with pink, against the leaden sky. Domination of horizontal, parallel lines. And the first wind-mill! As shaggy as a storm-tossed bird, it overhangs a hamlet of chalk-white and pale ochre houses: Goya's colours. Near Valdepeñas, pale red fallows and mauve hills, the very colours of Velázquez's *Coronation of the Virgin*. Low mud-coloured hovels of squalid villages suddenly shine like alabaster lamps when they become saturated with light in the bright peace of the evening, and all the window-panes—opaque sun-dazzled eyes at noontide—brighten up as if gushing with a myster-ious freshness: the pervasive gold of Zurbarán's *Apotheosis of St. Thomas*.

Now just as one can only imagine the milk-white baroque erection of the castle-convent of Melk among the pleasant Austrian hills, so nowhere else in the world but in stern, heat-baked Castille can our fantasy picture an Escorial. That Escorial which seemed so wearisome to the picturesque Théo, that he advised bored people to spend three or four days there: *"ils s'amuseront le reste de leur vie en pensant qu'ils pourraient être à l'Escurial et qu'ils n'y sont pas."* I do not know whether names always correspond to the nature of the things for which they stand, but I have little doubt but that, at least in past ages, the buildings seemed natural expressions of the landscapes in which they rose, and, just as a pearl is the quintessence of a shell, the building summed up the spirit of the country translated into number and measure by the maieutic intervention of man: architecture meant landscape become self-conscious.

Reflected by the rectangular pond of the gardens, the flank of the Escorial, with the numberless holes of its windows, is the perfect image of monotony. The eye glides along the sequel of gaps as a hand tells the beads of a rosary, to retrace its way backwards and then run again through the uniform row of little squares, dark green on the cold grey granite wall, while the pond reproduces on its staring surface that monumental cribbage-board. The echo which repeats the balanced call of the cuckoo in the "desert" of the Fontainebleau Forest does not convey half the sense of desperate solitude imparted by the silent echo of the pond reflecting the bare chequered pattern. It is as if the void were represented in terms of geometry, translated into intelligible signs for the human mind which recoils from the void. By going forwards and backwards, backwards and forwards, without a stop, through the rosary of the hundred equal windows, the mind plunges itself into—nothingness.

Was Philip the Second aiming at this, in order to forget the mouth of Hell gaping at his side, as in the nightmare painted by El Greco? Was it by counting with his disciplined eyes the rosary of little symmetrical squares that the nephew of Crazy Jane tried to lull and drug his troubled conscience, just as a sleepless man repeats the same word over and over again until his mind gets lost? From the farthermost corner of the choir in the church, did Philip the Second count the series of long organ-pipes, vertical and horizontal pipes, as inflexible as the angels' trumpets at Doomsday? Did he count the choir-stalls, upper and lower stalls, with the little columns all alike, one two, one two, one two, the similar arms, one two, one two, one two, and the heads of the canons as shiny as ivory balls, one two, one two, one two? . . .

The windows, the organ-pipes, the choir-stalls, the steps of the stairs, the suites of rooms, the fractions of the hours and days, to count all this, to count it again, to and fro, until one was freed from the terrific cetacean of the nightmare—its enormous

41

mouth teeming with tormented bodies—which came near every night, inexorably came near the bed of the supreme monarch of the faithful.

After all, is it not a similar state of disconsolate aridity peculiar to the dark night of the soul St. John of the Cross has described? To create a pneumatic void, to compress the conscience, whose usual course is a line, into an immovable, immaterial point; to try to achieve, in the completest absence of sensible things, the presence of the supersensible, to

> expresse
> A quintessence even from nothingnesse,
> From dull privations, and lean emptinesse . . .

Up to the production of the void one may say that Philip the Second succeeded. Did any of those happy moments come over him, which compensate the mystics for days and years of barren expectation? Did the arid soil split for the gush of a spring of water as blue as gentians blossoming on a crag? Days and years during which nothing happens, nothing but an incessant retelling of beads, while in that immense inane even the noise of a fly, or the boring of a worm in a distant piece of furniture, resound like peals of bells.

What more monotonous than the dark night of the soul, the mystic's state of waiting? No desire, no fear, no movement, not a single impulse; feeling anonymous, impersonal, the eye as set as a corpse's,

EL GRECO

Photo : Anderson

Dream of Philip II

42]

the spirit as vague and universal as the void or the absolute; a state of suspense in which one is dead to life and not yet born into bliss. Black on black, the same hieroglyph repeated numberless times, the staring surface of the soul reflecting the cribbage-board of prayer.

> Para venir a gustarlo todo,
> No quieras tener gusto en nada.
> Para venir a saberlo todo,
> No quieras saber algo en nada.
> Para venir a poseerlo todo,
> No quieras poseer algo en nada.
> Para venir a serlo todo,
> No quieras ser algo en nada.
> Para venir a lo que no gustas,
> Has de ir por donde no gustas.
> Para venir a lo que no sabes,
> Has de ir por donde no sabes.
> Para venir a lo que no posees,
> Has de ir por donde no posees.
> Para venir a lo que no eres,
> Has de ir por donde no eres . . .[1]

[1] San Juan de la Cruz, *Subida del Monte Carmelo*, Book I, Ch. xiii: "To attain enjoyment of all, seek to have enjoyment in nothing. To attain knowledge of all, seek to have knowledge of nothing in nothing. To attain possession of all, seek to have possession of nothing in nothing. To attain to be all, seek to be nothing in nothing. To attain what thou dost not enjoy, thou must go through where thou dost not enjoy. To attain what thou dost not know, thou must go through where thou dost not know. To attain what thou dost not possess, thou must go through where thou dost not possess. To attain what thou art not, thou must go through where thou art not."

Monotony is the very essence of the dark night of the soul; but this state of *"desnudez de espíritu,"* of interior hollowness, is the only state a mystic succeeds in describing to us. Since the unitive stage is ineffable, and, however tender and passionate and metaphysical the employed adjectives may be, the supreme expression of the mystical experience will always remain Jacopone's repetition to infinity, with more and more vehement intonation, of the same passionate word: *amore, amore . . .*; or even the repetition of the same ecstatic vowel, like the *A A A* uttered by Jeremiah after God had spoken to him.

" Hagamos de manera, que por medio de este ejercicio de amor ya dicho, lleguemos a vernos en tu *hermosura*; esto es, que seamos semejantes en *hermosura*, y sea tu *hermosura* de manera, que mirando el uno el otro se paresca a tí en tu *hermosura*, y se vea en tu *hermosura*; lo cual será transformándome a mí en tu *hermosura*; y así te veré yo a tí en tu *hermosura* y tú a mí en tu *hermosura*, y tú te verás en mí en tu *hermosura*, y yo me veré en tí en tu *hermosura*; y así paresca yo tú en tu *hermosura*, y paresca tú yo en tu *hermosura*, y mi *hermosura* sea tu *hermosura*, y tu *hermosura* mi *hermosura*, y seré yo tú en tu *hermosura*, y serás tú yo en tu *hermosura*, porque tu *hermosura* mesma será mi hermosura." [1]

[1] San Juan de la Cruz, *Cántico Espíritual*, commentary on the

Photo : A. Caröe

THE WALLS OF ÁVILA

Few readings are therefore more monotonous than mystical literature, and anthologies of mystics show no more variety than one would find in a bunch of sunflowers. *Ab uno disce omnes*. No wonder, then, that the Castilian soul has found her supreme ex‑pression in mysticism, and that one of the greatest mystics was born by the stumpiest and earthiest walls of the stumpiest and earthiest of peninsulas: I mean St. Teresa of Avila.

For—may it be a casual circumstance, I wonder? —is it not remarkable that Italy, the most varied country in the world, should have such an indented, lively outline, a slenderness which nearly gives her the profile of an intelligent being, there in the middle of the blue Latin sea, while Spain, similar to the spread bull‑hide with which she was compared by Strabo, looks thickset, geometrical, pentagonal?

second line of stanza xxxv: "Let us act in such way that by means of this exercise of love we may attain to see each other in thy beauty; that is to say, that we may be alike in beauty, and that thy beauty may be such that one of us, looking at the other, may resemble thee in thy beauty and see himself in thy beauty; and this will come to pass by my being transformed into thy beauty; and thus shall I see thee in thy beauty, and thou wilt see me in thy beauty, and thou wilt see thyself in me in thy beauty, and I shall see myself in thee in thy beauty; in such a way that I shall appear like to thee in thy beauty, and thou wilt appear like to me in thy beauty, and that my beauty may be thy beauty and thy beauty my beauty, and I shall be thou in thy beauty, and thou wilt be myself in thy beauty, because thy very beauty will be my beauty."

which in no way differs from an average Spanish puzzle play developed according to the rules of a consummate and crystallised art of conversation. The comparison of life to a dream had been expounded by the Greek tragedians with a far greater depth and a much statelier verse centuries before Calderón's half-witted Sigismundo rehearsed it in this almost Metastasian *canzonetta*:

Yo sueño que estoy aquí
Destas prisiones cargado,
Y soñé que en otro estado
Mas lisonjero me ví.
¿Qué es la vida?—Un frenesí—
¿Qué es la vida?—Un ilusión—
Una sombra, une ficción,
Y el mayor bien es pequeño:
Que toda *la vida es sueño*
Y los sueños sueño son.[1]

Calderón, however, was of Flemish descent from

[1] Act II, Sc. xviii. D. F. Mac-Carthy's translation of this passage runs:

'Tis a dream that I in sadness
Here am bound, the scorn of fate;
'Twas a dream that once a state
I enjoyed of light and gladness.
What is life? 'Tis but a madness.
What is life? A thing that seems,
A mirage that falsely gleams,
Phantom joy, delusive rest,
Since is life a dream at best,
And even dreams themselves are dreams.

his mother's side. Here is perhaps the reason why he wrote only a hundred and twenty dramas, eighty *autos,* and about twenty more theatrical pieces. Had also his mother been Spanish, who knows whether Lope would bear the palm of fertility?

But, Gil Blas, I hear your querulous voice: *"O divin Lope de Vega, rare et sublime génie, et vous moëlleux Calderón, dont la douceur élégante et purgée d'épique est inimitable, ne craignez point tous deux que vos autels soient abattus. . . ."*

*   *   *   *   *

Spaniards are a happy nation—G. K. Chesterton once remarked—but they eat rather on the principle of the boa constrictor: an enormous meal, followed by lethargy. On the symposial capacities of this nevertheless frugal nation little doubt can be entertained by anyone acquainted with Spain. What one finds surprising is the monotony of their banquets. Even Baedeker warns you: "The food is usually good and plentiful, though somewhat monotonous." Should one see in this habit an unmistakable sign of Roman extraction? But Trimalchio took pains only about the most picturesque dainties: feathered hares surrounded with sow heads, boars stuffed with thrushes, pies of nightingale tongues, and similar delicacies, either indigenous or exotic, were required to interest his palate. Now far be it from me to offer any disparagement of the *paella*

valenciana and the *puchero*, those rustic encyclo‑
pædias of savours where each savour suffers elision.
I understand how one can gourmandise to the point
of agony on such clownish fare, in a moment of
bucolic nostalgia, or even mystical aspiration, since,
on the authority of St. Teresa, "*entre los pucheros
anda el Señor.*" But what should one say of the
eternal stewed or roast meat, of the excellent but
inevitable *chuletas de cerdo* or *de ternero*, of the veget‑
able soups where the hot and windy *garbanzo* (the
Latin *cicer*) holds its court, of the perverse and tough
bacalao, of the praiseworthy but invariable *huevos
fritos* and *tortillas*? How can the palate be content
with a daily recurrence of the same dishes? And,
above all, how can one tolerate, day in and day out,
a joint visit of all the dishes known to Spanish
cookery? The more so, if there were truth in what
Madame d'Aulnoy had heard about seventeenth‑
century Spain: "Everything is so nourishing here,
that an egg profits you more than a pigeon else‑
where; I think it is an effect of the climate." O
exquisite epicures on whom even snipe bids fair to
pall, let alone the ever‑recurring partridge, what
would you do in the country of "*toujours poischiche,*"
where the struggle for life is called *lucha por gar‑
banzos*?

The same monotony as one notices in Spanish
meals becomes alarming in public spectacles. The

most picturesque of all not excepted, *"las fiestas más famosas y típicas del mundo; estas fiestas nuestras únicas por su luz y colores incomparables, y donde el fervor religioso va unido a un bello sentimiento de paganía,"* [1] I mean the famous Sevillian Holy Week, a spectacle so unique, that the inn-keepers ask double price for the occasion, and do not allow the curious foreigner to leave until the classic cycle of seven days is concluded. To the Spaniards seven days do not seem too many: Seville is a *maravilla*, a marvel, and those seven days are seven wonders; even if the days of festivity were more, the interest of the Spaniards would not flag. Should the Holy Week be as long as Lent, it is a fair surmise that the Spaniards would enjoy their daily pageant all the same.

In the first rank of the seats disposed in Plaza de la Constitución, one sees them on Palm Sunday, those picturesque-hunting foreigners, mostly English and Americans, waiting from three o'clock in the after-noon, in the already hot and hard April sunlight, for the procession scheduled for about half-past seven. Alice, the Broadway blonde, newly arrived in this Wonderland, is all agog with expectation. If

---

[1] The most famous and typical festivities of the world; those festivities of ours so unique on account of their incomparable light and colours; where the religious enthusiasm goes hand in hand with a fine sense of paganism.

she can read Spanish, she reads in the programme of something intriguing called *saetas* and *piropos "que brotan espontáneos y sinceros al paso de un Crucificado o de una bella Dolorosa que pone temblores y congojos en las almas."* [1] So those processions are going to give her a thrill. Meanwhile the sun is pretty hot, but is one not supposed to enjoy the Sevillian sun? Besides, the crowd is so picturesque! Every woman is Carmen, every man Don Juan. The rows of chairs gradually get filled, the cries of the *aguadores* and *gaseosa*-vendors become more frequent, the tribune of the Ayuntamiento turns black with fashionable people, those fascinating Sevillian señoras, dressed just as in the movies, so cute, so vampish! A sudden row; what is the matter? Is the procession already there? No, it is only a child's red air-balloon hanging loose in the blue sky. The southern crowd is so excitable, so picturesque! It's bully!

The hours go by. "Have some monkey nuts?" When the pavement is well littered with nutshells and orange-peel, the first squad of *guardia civil* appears at the entrance of Sierpes, blowing their trumpets. The mounted police look fine: a whole party of Napoleons, with tight knee-breeches, laced hats, impassive faces. "So different from our traffic

---

[1] Which burst out spontaneous and sincere at the passage of a Crucifix or a beautiful Mater Dolorosa who sets the soul shuddering and sobbing.

cops ! '' And here are the Nazarenes with tall
conical head-dresses, and hoods pulled down over
their faces, pacing slowly into the square. Look at
the maces, and the banner, and the *paso*! The sacred
float, the Sagrada Cena Sacramental, is carried on
the shoulders of so many men who every now and
then stop to ventilate their heads twisted with a pro-
fessional stiff neck. "Say, do look at that kid balanc-
ing his huge conical hat and holding his little candle
aslant, isn't he cute?" Next comes a glittering array
of candles, and the baldaquin of Nuestra Señora del
Subterráneo, with the military band behind boom-
ing out a funeral march. The *paso* comes to a stand-
still, and a nasal voice intones a shrill monotonous
wail, which suddenly breaks down, among the
chuckles of the crowd. It is the *saeta*, the famous
saeta, whoopee! What a swell procession! Pity it
is already half-past eight, and one has to hustle back
to the hotel. Dinner is sure to be heralded by a cock-
tail sol y sombra, which has such a toreadoric smack!

On the next day the Broadway blonde cannot
keep quiet until evening comes, and the rows of
chairs turn black with people, and the melancholy
cries of the *aguadores* and *gaseosa*-vendors punctuate
the confused chattering of the crowd, and Nuestro
Jesús de las Penas and Nuestra Señora de los Dolores
appear at the entrance of Sierpes. . . . The crowd
seems to be always laughing at the *saeta*-singers:

should one believe that sceptical Sevillian friend who confidentially has hinted that those *saetas* and *piropos* so "spontaneous and sincere" are paid by the Corporation in order to impress foreigners? "You aren't a bit sentimental!"—Alice, with amused eyes behind the horn-rimmed glasses, has said reproachfully to the sleek Don José. Don José is a chivalrous fellow, but not too generous; anyway it won't ruin him to show them around and buy them all those little cups of that monotonous wine, *manzanilla* they called it, that unexciting *manzanilla* wine, with those uninteresting paraphernalia of fried sardines and anchovies twisted round a moderately appetising tooth-pick! Yes, very picturesque for the first time, but not half as expensive as those delicious cocktails in her club at home. Anyway, he has promised them that coveted dainty, the tails of the bulls with haricot beans *a la andaluza*, a very special speciality, for which you had to hunt through half Seville.

On holy Wednesday Alice gives up marking with a cross in the time-table of the *confradías* the passage of each *paso*. Why, how is it possible to remember what the Santísimo Cristo de la Misericordia looks like, or how he is to be distinguished from the Santísimo Cristo del Buen Fin and the Santísimo Cristo de la Salud, since the three Christs are as like as peas? So they might as well be missed out.

54

At three o'clock p.m. sharp on holy Thursday the Cardinal Archbishop washes the feet of twelve poor people in the Cathedral transept. Since two o'clock the tourists have crowded the first row of seats. They have taken with them good field-glasses so that not even a corn of the pseudo-apostles' feet should escape their eyes eager for picturesqueness. That is going to be great fun! Then, from five p.m. to eight o'clock the next morning, Friday, there are a lot of processions to be watched, seven churches to be visited, Eslava's grand Miserere to be heard, the famous Madrugada to be attended, *los funerales* to be enjoyed. . . . It is going to be wonderful!

The visit to the seven churches is "a wow." Sevillian ladies have very diminutive feet—"such bad legs, anyhow, most of them"—and doll's eyes, just cute little mascot's eyes, too quaint; they sit in the churches at the counter of the offerings, just to jingle the duros, while all the young bucks in the shadow of the aisles devour them with their eyes. They are onto the women, the Spaniards! The Broadway blonde, if she has been wise enough to purchase an authentic Sevillian outfit complete with a tortoise-shell comb made in New York and a silk shawl manufactured in Lyons, now reaps the fruit of her disguise in the form of the killing glances which the dandies cast at her rather than at the genuine *majas*, thanks to the exotic touch in her countenance. However, after having gone through the churches and coveted just a bit of the gold and silver lace of the Madonnas to bring back home as a souvenir (there would be a dash of sacrilege in cutting that fringe with scissors, if one had a pair of them handy!), after having rubbed herself against the thick hedges of Don Juans, Alice feels creepy all over: "Oh, how positively disgusting, look!"— a flea, an authentic fat Spanish flea. Alice wonders whether she ought to go into hysterics, but she decides she has no time to spare. A blast of trumpets on her right. Is it the Santísimo Cristo de la Exaltación or Nuestro Padre Jesús Atado a la Columna? Pounding of drums on her left. Candles here, more candles there, and conical hats every‹ where. Then the funeral march breaks out, as usual. The first *paso* is always a Christ, the second always a Madonna, and there is no end to them: a Christ, a Madonna, a Christ, a Madonna. . . .

Alice feels that it would be a great thing if it were already Saturday morning, but how can she possibly admit that she is bored? This depressing thought is probably caused by the not‹very‹comfortable edge of the Colón monument, in the Cathedral, against which she is leaning as well as she can, since the chairs offered by that horrid dago, the verger, for twenty pesetas each, have been emphatically waved away by father. But the notes of Eslava's grand

Miserere soon thunder melodramatically in the aisles, and she cheers up and observes with renewed interest the bare feet of the last Nazarenes who are slowly shuffling along; she squeezes into the procession—it is as good as being at a meeting of the Ku⁄Klux⁄Klan—until she feels a sticky burning sweet⁄ness on her neck (is it a kiss? these southerners under⁄stand working around the ladies!) and by touch she finds a crisp drop of wax, and more wax blobs—yellow, white, black ones—she discovers on herself here and there, so that her pink frock, in which she looks so cute, is quite ruined.

Now the Cathedral is emptying of people, and Alice with her exhausted parents rushes to the Pasaje de Oriente, where poppa and mamma try to buck themselves up with so much whisky, that by midnight poppa feels like bed, and daughter with a few strenuous friends walks to Plaza San Lorenzo to take up a position for the spectacle of two o'clock in the morning, the Salida del Cristo del Gran Poder. How many cigarettes does she smoke be⁄tween midnight and two o'clock? She, too, feels like bed, but how can she dare to confess it? She had hungered to see this Madrugada for years. There⁄fore to the questions of her friends she keeps ready a smiling: "I just love it!" At last all lights are put out in the jammed square, and the main portal is thrown wide open on a vista of thousands of candles.

It is just divine! Click go a hundred cameras which have been on the watch for the black silhouette of the Christ waveringly advancing in front of the lights. Here he is, Nuestro Padre Jesús del Gran Poder, with his black-veiled head shaggy with thorns and rays; his cross is like a huge X. "Have you gotten him?"—"Yes, ma'am: this is going to be a swell picture."—"Fine! And now, let's get a move on and go to the Alameda de Hercules to meet the Macarena! Never mind those *saetas*; they are just the same sort of mush everywhere."

A blast of trumpets on the left, pounding of drums on the right. Alice, dog-tired, enters a café with her friends to have a drink. Is it her head which is wobbly, or are those soldiers dressed like Romans, round the statue of the Macarena, actually lurching like a troop of drunkards?

About six o'clock in the morning we find Alice sitting with her friends outside the Cathedral; they all look tired as after a necking party, and no less sleepy than the surrounding crowd of town and country people. After an aimless rambling through the little squares of the Barrio de la Cruz shimmer-ing in the moonlight, the party of Yankees have accepted the offer of the chair-attendant who exalted his clean chairs: "*¡No hay chinches!*" And, while sitting, they shiver at the peep of dawn, and, as in a nightmare, they see—the Jesús del Gran

A *Paso*

Poder, again, and the Macarena, again—exactly similar to the other Madonnas—and Nuestro Padre Jesús de las Tres Caídas and Nuestro Padre Jesús de la Salud, swaying along so slowly, among the last straggling Nazarenes who carry their candles aslant, eager to leave the procession at the Cathedral gates, those gates closed to the shivering public outside.

"O, isn't this thing ever going to stop?" But, honestly, how could one go back to America without being able to tell that one had seen the Santísimo Cristo de la Salud, the Santísimo Cristo de la Expiración, the Santísimo Cristo de la Conversión del Buen Ladrón, Nuestro Padre Jesús Descendido de la Cruz en el Misterio de Su Sagrada Mortaja, and Maria Santísima de la Luz en el Misterio de Sus Tres Necesidades, Nuestra Señora del Mayor Dolor en Su Soledad, Nuestra Señora del Patrocinio, Nuestra Señora de Montserrat, and, most of all, Nuestra Señora de la O? Now, how could one? Because Alice knows perfectly well, by now, that behind the most romantic, improbable names is hidden the same Madonna with a pudding-like crown and a gorgeous trailing mantle, leaning over a lot of candles, the whole float swaying on the shoulders of thirty to forty tipsy bearers, and followed by the melancholy rumble of funereal trombones: she knows all this very well, but can she dare to tell her friends? To be fixed up to go to Spain six months beforehand, to have come all the way from New York—just to confess that, after all, that famous Holy Week looked more beautiful in Cook's prospectuses, and that those mysterious complaints, which sounded so thrilling in the gramophone records, those mystic *saetas*, were, sure, a rather poor affair, no more romantic than the screams of whacked niggers—how could one honestly confess all this? It would be awful. And, after all, even the sceptical Sevillian friend, for all his making a mock of certain features of the Holy Week programme (under the picture of a naked scourged Christ one read the engaging invitation: *"Un precioso pantalón fantasía encarguelo en la Gran Sastrería Española, Gran Capitán 18"* [1]), even Don José put on a serious face, when one of the Yankees had dared to call in question the variety of the spectacle. Foreigners could not understand; every sacred image awoke in an Andalusian mind a different group of associations with which a foreigner would never be familiar. All those similar Christs were in reality as so many different divinities, and each of them boasted his jealous devotees, who exalted him over all the others. To call such a spectacle monotonous, what a blasphemy! Those foreigners had really no philosophy in them! Since every new dish of *garbanzos* is a different dish;

[1] Order a superb pair of fancy trousers at the Great Spanish Tailor's, Gran Capitán 18.

FRANCISCO RIZI   *Photo : J. Ruiz Vernacci*

Charles II and his Court at the Spectacular *Auto-da-Fé* of June 30th, 1680, in the Plaza Mayor of Madrid

On the left is assembled the Holy Office. The heretics, in their sanbenitos, are being led from the right to the platform in the centre, for the preliminary religious formalities, then to another (here invisible) part of the square to the stake. The atmosphere prevailing in this portion of the scene is that of a state reception.

[60]

nay, each *garbanzo* is a different, unique *garbanzo*, as in the sky the similar-looking stars are each of them a different world. How could foreigners appreciate the sublime question of that Spanish king who, after having watched from five to six dozen *auto-da-fé's*, had asked: "*¿Hay más?*" (Any more?) among the cheers of the edified clergy? Had not Charles the Second spent a whole day, from sunrise to sunset, in the Plaza Mayor of Madrid, to see a hundred heretics burnt alive? For the vulgar herd every new smell of burnt flesh would have been a smell of burnt flesh and nothing more, but the nostrils of His Catholic Majesty were likely to distinguish a whole scale of smells, from singeing to roasting, according to the different heresies of the people undergoing religious treatment.

Perhaps the Sevillian friend was right: only Spaniards could thoroughly enjoy the processions. But, surely, she would not get bored by the grand Easter bull-fight: something like *Sangre y Arena* with Rudolph Valentino in it, but, instead of a mere film, real palpitating life, how thrilling! So Alice thought, while she caressed in her fingers the green ticket, with a rough picture on it of a bull-fighter borne in triumph on the shoulders of the *aficionados*, and in the centre, in blood-red letters, the word: SOMBRA.

Once inside the humming bull-ring, through the tiers solid with olive-skinned people in black clothes (what has happened to the coloured shawls?)—Alice savouring as she passes their wild smell—the party of Americans twist their way toward their seats. They reach them just in time. For, with an unspeakable mixture of horror and delight, Alice sees a man tossed on the horns of the bull, and in that man she recognises the bull-fighter who is staying at her hotel, and in a flash she sees again the comings and goings of *aficionados* who had been ushered by the policeman into the hero's room during the hours before the bull-fight, all dressed in black, all as obsequious as clergymen, with such glances showing all the white of their eyes—a roomful of dark men, so thrilling, so thrilling!—and she sees HIM coming out of the shadow of the room, a pattern of gold, as solemn as if he were having his shoes blacked; all this she sees again in a flash, and she sees the sallow cock-eyed youth who wished luck to the torero in the doorway, while the panic-stricken porter muttered: *"¡Jesús! ¡Es tuerto!"*—and she remembers the words of her Sevillian friend who explained to her the ominous implication—oh, it is so thrilling to see those forebodings come true, now (she had sensed it!), and, surely, in the twinkling of an eye the wax-pale bull-fighter expires in the arms of a dark Carmen, in a roomful of men all dressed in black who cross themselves and cast their eyes up, eyes with enormous whites in the olive faces!

But no, the bull-fighter gets to his feet and limps out of the arena, supported by his assistants. No, he is not going to die; the Sevillian friend fancies he is making her breathe freely by saying that the wounds are very light, in fact, not dangerous at all, they will not prevent him from taking part in next corrida. (To her friends at home it will be better to write that the torero has received a death-wound.) Any-way, there is still hope of seeing a really dead man before the end of the spectacle. Meanwhile the mad bull—but how small that bull looks! she had thought he would be double the size of a buffalo—the bull makes straight for the horses standing over against the barrier. What, that thing a mad bull? Not on your life! No, there's no "pep" in him, but as for the men, they are "peppy" enough to make up for it, while they wave their capes as pink as the lamp-shades in a dining-car! But never mind, here is blood, and—how horrible! that dark coral necklace hanging out from below the horse's belly. How . . . how lovely!—exclaims the fascinated girl hysteri-cally. This is really Spain, chivalric Spain. If one could only get hold of some delicious stiff drink, just to face up the situation with that rather wonder-ful creepy feeling down the spine! But poppa, oh, poppa is not a sport, poppa, that tall man with a powerful chin—who would have imagined it?— poppa turns sallow and looks rigidly in front of him, poppa looks funny, and obviously is going to be sick; until, after a painful pause, he declares, as if something had dawned upon him at last: "Now I understand why Spaniards are not a civilised race!" Poppa springs to his feet to leave the bull-ring. But daughter entreats him to wait at least until the death of the bull.

As for the first bull, she doesn't do so badly. Two horses spilled open, a torero wounded (*nearly mortally*), and, finally, the bull killed, but only at the third sword thrust, it is true, and after having thrown up blood amid the disapproving cries of the crowd. Anyhow, a spectacle to give you a sudden turn, just what the Broadway blonde is after. A blast of trumpets, and the second bull dashes in. A whisper: "*¡Chiquito, muy chiquito!*" is heard all round. Indeed it is a shame, the Sevillian friend explains, it is all but indecent to put in the ring a diminutive bull like that; the Marqués de Villamarina does not enhance his reputation with his cattle. He is quite a nice bull, though—and here is a horse gored, here are the *capeadores* taking cover behind the *burladeros*, in short, it's like the tension before the catastrophe. Now comes the turn of the *banderilleros*, and the three usual pairs of frilled darts are seen ornamenting the bulls' shoulder, just like the frill of a Wiener Schnitzel. And now comes the *espada*! He holds out the *muleta*, pirouettes with joined heels close to the bull's head. Such a silly animal, to keep ducking his horns at the rag, instead of at the man; why isn't he just the least little bit vicious? "At him!"—she is aching to shout. But the bull lets the amateurish *espada* drive one after the other three swords into his neck, as if it were a sort of pin-cushion, and finally settles down and— no, he is not dead, he is just thinking things over with himself. He hasn't any kick left. Half the crowd stands up, protesting against the bull's fit of introspection; and here they come again, the *capea- dores*, flicking their pink lampshades almost under the nose of the placid animal, who finally staggers to his feet again and with stoical resignation presents to the *espada* his dilapidated neck for the final stab. *And den he fall down go boom!*

But poppa is quite upset, poppa is going to leave the arena together with mamma. Alice feels her parental respect considerably sinking. Just think of the admiration she had felt for poppa when he had pushed a loaded revolver under the nose of the im- pertinent nigger valet—over there, at home—that impertinent buck nigger who was gallivanting with a white maid servant, ugh! And now a little mess up of a horse and bull was enough to bowl him over! Oh, poppa, who would have imagined it, you with your powerful chin, such a fine energetic he-man! And just while poppa has gotten to his feet and tries

E   65

to shove through the indignant Spaniards ("What a sissy!"—they must think), just at that moment an aeroplane booms over the arena dropping advertisements, and poppa, looking the very spirit of Service, grabs the arm of the next man dressed in black, and with a grimace of disgust, pointing out the bull who is being dragged out by a jangling mule team, cries out: "Yesterday!"—then he turns his face to the sky, with a radiant smile which displays a glittering set of gold teeth, and points to the aeroplane: "*¡Mañana!*" Then, very dignified, he turns his back on the puzzled and sneering bystanders, leaving them to brood over the lofty meaning of his brief inspirational speech in which he has summed up two different worlds and civilisations. Poppa was grand; but just a bit too much like the Rev. MacCracken delivering his Special Revival Sunday Message at the First Free United Episcopal Methodist Grand Basilica.

Piebald like a papier-mâché cow, the third bull seemed to watch the tarantella of the *banderilleros* in a spirit of amused detachment. In vain the *picadores* shoved the horses' bellies quite close to his head for the horn injection; the bull grazed them rather fastidiously, and then wheeled round snuffing very gently. The crowd was amusing, anyway: they had become furiously energetic. Her Sevillian friend, for instance, was wildly gesticulating, and rolling his

eyes, and pulling his hair, and uttering incoherent sounds as if the whole business reflected discredit on him personally. And all over the bull⸝ring there was an excited waving of handkerchiefs, an angry shout⸝ing towards the President's box, an isolated, then a universal roar: "¡Al redondel! ¡Echarse al redondel!"
—while in the arena the banderilla⸝dancers con⸝tinued to whirl round the phlegmatic animal, with⸝out much conviction, however. And then some⸝thing extraordinary happened. The corral gate was thrown open and two gawky white steers straddled in slowly, dangling their bells, like pictures of cows on Swiss chocolate wrappers, and the bull, how killing! followed them, just as in England men meekly follow the wives by whom they are hauled out of the pub on a Saturday night. Yes, very funny, but where were death and fate and the Andalusian fire, where was the pep? At the fourth bull one felt that some grand splash of activity was decidedly overdue to put the show to rights, and indeed, after the usual administration of thrusts and punctures, the bull was faced by an awfully smart *espada*, who began a series of acrobatic contortions and elaborate genuflections under the bull's muzzle. The bull charged with two or three bounds, then stopped short, turned, and recharged with two or three bounds in the opposite direction, like a clock⸝work toy. "Isn't he a lamb?" The effect of this was to

split up the spectators into two parties, for terrific
¡ole! rose from one side, and hisses from the other,
while the Sevillian friend tried to explain to Alice
that "*esas contracciones retorcidas, esas quebraduras de
cintura, esas cosas tan raras que hace, francamente aquí
no resultan, aquí no agradan, aquí no gustan. Hay que
torear con naturalidad.*" [1] So all this was not the right
sort of thing, wasn't it? The too fussy *espada*, anyway, was able to *descabellar* at the first blow, so that
the ¡ole! rose to the sky, and the caps of the *aficionados* were showered on the ring. A rare thing, Alice
is told, to kill the bull at the first go. It is all very
well, but she cannot help remembering that she has
experienced a much stronger emotional feeling
when watching two trains smash and telescope each
other at a garden party organised to help the Christian Science fund, or when admiring Douglas Fair-
banks while he took a plunge from an aeroplane
upside down onto a train dashing over a blazing
bridge spanning a waterfall. No, the bull-fight has
so far failed to tickle her to death, nor is it likely to
do so with the four last bulls. Certainly not with
the fifth one who shows a propensity to leap into the
gangway, so that the bull-ring attendants are obliged

[1] These twisted contractions, these leanings on the side, these
quaint things he does, frankly do not come off here, have no
appeal here, are not liked here. One must be natural in bull-
fighting.

to vault to and fro first into the arena, and then into the gangway, every time the bull leaps back. And the sixth one, after bounding into the ring in a rather melodramatic way, what should he do but set the public protesting! *"Es tuerto"*—the Sevillian friend explains, rather indignantly,—*"es tuerto :hay algo raro y blancuzco en el ojo izquierdo."* "O yes, I see!" She sees nothing, for all her keeping her eyes glued on the bull's head. That eye must be a sure enough miracle. But how can one possibly see from such a distance whether the bull has gotten a squint, whether there is something whitish in his eye? The bull is dispatched amid a chorus of insults of the crowd, maybe at the fourth sword thrust. The last bull would hardly have been more exciting, but for a blunder of the *espada* who struck him in the wrong place between the horns : the public hissed the torero and applauded the victim. "It isn't fair, of course it isn't fair!"—Alice agreed when she had it explained. *"¡Fué mucha corridita!"*—declared the Sevillian friend—*"Una corrida soporífera, aburridísima e insulsa. Nunca el caudal del aburrimiento es tan grande, tan portentoso y tan anfiteátrico como en los toros."* [1] No pep in it, no go. It wasn't fair to kill the bull so perfunctorily, without giving him a dog's chance of charging into the man, it wasn't fair to bring in

[1] The amount of boredom is never so big, so portentous, so amphitheatrical, as in bull-fights.

diminutive bulls, which even a kiddy might stroke between the horns, while they, no doubt, would lick his hand like lap-dogs, how disgusting, how little virile, "how little *veronal*, don't you say so, here?"— oh, yes, of course, *varonil*: it was the weariness of the show which made her say *veronal*: so sleepy! It wasn't fair, it positively wasn't, to set a girl's fancy working with pictures of a life intense and thrilling, life in the raw, of handsome men killed, dark vampish señoras, dusky dishevelled Carmens, blood, sand, hell, destiny, death, and all peppy and creepy things, to fob her off with a sort of uneventful butchery, a loathsome butchery, in which the most interesting episodes were supplied by the wrong things, the things which should never take place, the steers, the squint in the eye, the matador's un-natural contortions, and all that sort of thing—if only they had given a demonstration of those *banderillas de fuego* with the consequent smell of grill-room, or of those mysterious *perros* to which her guide-book alluded!

The romance of the corrida was utterly spoilt; another shattered illusion. Were it possible, the American girl would sue the impresario, the bulls, the bull-fighters, the public, the whole of Spain, for obtaining money under false pretences. No, it wasn't fair at all, it certainly wasn't!

DU SANG, DE LA VOLUPTÉ, DE LA MORT

DU SANG, DE LA VOLUPTÉ,
DE LA MORT

Dass ihr doch wenigstens als Thiere vollkom-
men wäret! Aber zum Thiere gehört die Un-
schuld—NIETZSCHE

Now do not think that the bull-fight I have just described is a travesty. Rather, it is a typical bull-
fight, with the difference that the average bull-fight
is a much more monotonous affair. You will not
always find, to animate it, the episode of the cabe-
stros or the somersault of the torero who lets himself
be gored by mistake; though you will hardly miss
the hullabaloo of the public protesting against the
inevitable bull suspected of squinting. Of course,
in ever so many hundreds of bull-fights, you are
bound to get one masterpiece. As for this latter,
happy indeed those who have seen it: they will
transmit its account to the generations to come.

The romantic reader may read the description of
a theoretically ideal corrida in Gautier; such a treat
indeed, this one, that whoever, after him, has written
on bull-fights, has generally borrowed the showiest
colours from the rich palette of picturesque Théo.
It is a well-known fact, for instance, that Théo
was so largely exploited by the author of *Cuore*
(whose lachrymal apparatus, so sensitive as a rule,

73

refused to work in front of the horse, and bull, slaughter), that *his* description of a bull-fight is quoted as a typical instance of plagiarism. Can we honestly call De Amicis to account, once we hear that Gautier, too, has based his description on a previous one, which, in its turn, we may safely guess to have been drawn from the letters of that fantastic Madame d'Aulnoy, who, by the end of the seven, teenth century first discovered (or among the first, since Corneille also has a claim in this connection) the romance of Iberian exoticism? Madame d'Aul, noy, however, took her description, word for word, from a letter of Carel de Sainte,Garde . . . And here I think it wise to stop, but I surmise that this tradi, tional bull,fight portraiture goes back to an age immemorial.

I grant—Ramón Pérez de Ayala will say—that bull,fights are monotonous, barbarous, revolting, and silly, but there is a *quid divinum* which causes them to be, after all, beautiful.

A *quid divinum*. Quite so, the great Spanish writer will continue to say, bull,fights are something more than an institution: they are an actual propitiatory sacrifice offered to the divinity, just like a religious ceremony. Even the bull,fighters' dress reminds one of the Byzantine sensuousness of ecclesiastical vest, ments: it is that *parentesco de dorados* which another Ramón, Ramón Gómez de la Serna, has recently

GOYA

74]

Corrida

emphasised in *El torero Caracho*. For this younger
Ramón, too, the bull-fight is *seria como fiesta en patio
de sacramental*. The bull stands for the high altar,
the torero is similar to a bishop, or, rather, to a
Christian martyr, to a statue of St. Francis, to Velázquez's Christ, to Christ on the Mount of Olives: he
wears the cape as a chasuble, and with his muleta
makes *unos signos de última bendición*.

I confess that I find Ayala's fine essay, in *Política y
toros*, so captivating with its authoritative grace,
that, after reading it, I nearly felt impelled to change
my mind; were it not that another writer, a Frenchman, has recently enlarged upon the Spaniard's
opinion in a book, and, through his excess of zeal,
has imperilled a thesis which, though deceptive,
was, however, suavely plausible in Ayala's essay.

I am not sure whether pan-taurism is a sort of religion or rather a psychical complex; be it as it may,
Viscount Henri de Montherlant has the merit of
having been the first to formulate it in *Les Bestiaires*.[1]

---

[1] I quote the passages of *Les Bestiaires* from the English
translation of Edwin Gile Rich (*The Bullfighters*, London, Cape,
1928), whenever their raciness has not been lost in the translation, a thing which, alas, happens only too frequently. The
jacket of the English edition contains the following notice, which
readers of my Introduction will find characteristic enough:
"*The Bullfighters* is a story of Spain, . . . in a vivid atmosphere of
romance and danger (the italics are mine). It ends with a great
bull-fight, which the author treats in a spectacular manner."

Pan-taurism can be defined as a sort of ecstasy or delirium in consequence of which the world is conceived under the appearance of taurinity, *sub specie taurinitatis*, the name given to it by its formulator being *transe taurine*.

The tendency to pan-taurism is early apprehended through a violent pro-Spanish feeling. The subject begins by experiencing an irrepressible craving to appear Spanish, and to this effect he combs his hair with a lead comb in order to make it look darker, adopts a Cordovan felt hat for his head-dress, covers his fingers with diamond rings, has his boots polished at every step, drinks Anis del Mono, and, whenever it is on, goes to hear the opera of *Carmen*, whose overture makes him beside himself. All these fixed ideas belong to the symptomatological equipment of pan-taurism. The very sound of the Spanish language acts on the subject as the sight of a desirable courtesan. The very sight of Spanish women takes his breath away and thrills him to the point of shrieking. In order to be a Spanish woman it is necessary to dress in black, to have a hair dark as the plumage of a crow, and a pale face apt to assume a halo-like radiance against that compact blackness as if against the bituminous background of an old painting. Before long, as mere libido appears to be a thing too obvious and commonplace, it is succeeded by a more complex and delicate feeling. The subject becomes aware of such an acute sense of delight in the act of beating his beloved, as to beggar description. *Les sévices font leur fleur en amour* becomes one of his principles, while another runs: "A man can really conquer only what he loves, and conquerors are tremendous lovers." *Qui plus castigat plus amore ligat*. Therefore, no end of spanking!

Up to this point, one might logically infer a variety of sadism. But sadism itself is an affection too obvious and commonplace; besides, it is by no means easy to gratify it normally without drawing to oneself the unasked-for attention of the law. In short, the subject perceives that it is decidedly impracticable to decorate one's pedestal every night with the head of the beloved neatly severed from her trunk, as in Baudelaire's *Une Martyre*. Then a process of symbolical transference takes place in him, similar to those expounded by Freud. Namely, woman, *qua* object of libido, becomes identified with the bed; Latin for bed is *torus*, and, surprisingly enough, *taurus* is Latin for bull. The two words are evidently related. "It is astonishing how much a bed resembles a bull." Once put on this way, the subject goes inevitably through all the stages of the *transe taurine*, or pan-taurism. The bed stands for the woman, the bull for the bed; *ergo*, woman is a bull, and, *e converso*, a bull is practically identical with a woman. To kill a bull becomes then a transposition of the sexual act, since the matador's sword seems indeed endowed with *la puissance virile*: once thrust into the body of the bull, it draws from it *l'énergie génératrice* and makes it pass into the killer's body. The subject approaches a bull *"comme on rapproche une femme qu'on va faire entrer dans sa chair."*

But before giving his affection a direct outlet by taking part in an actual bull-fight, the subject goes through an intermediate stage, characterised by the persistence of the original elements. He is "fasci= nated by his bed." He sees in the bed the form of a bull, with his very horns, legs, tail: *c'est tout à fait cela*. The very thing. During this phase the subject indulges in such practices as the one described here below:

"Alban closed the shutters so that he could not be seen from outside, and pushed the furniture against the walls. In one hand he held a ruler, in the other a muleta. Obviously the bull had little spirit left, so he must be finished quickly. A few passes (which unfortunately sent the crockery flying) and Alban encouraged himself in a loud voice: 'Bueno . . . bueno. . . .' Then he profiled,[1] and like a good

[1] The French has *se profile*. It is a technical word of bull= fighting, rendered by Hemingway (*Fiesta*, pp. 252–3) with *to profile*. Mr. E. G. Rich's translation, *stood sideways*, is wrong.

matador, without turning his head, slew his eider‹
down."

However, this kind of solitary gratification in the
long run palls on him; the subject wants an actual
bull, a bloody *taurus*:

"Ce qui le tourmentait alors, c'était d'être privé de
la décharge nerveuse que procure la lame qui s'en‹
fonce, c'était cette anxiété de la chose pas consom‹
mée qui épuise les toucheurs de jeunes filles. . . .
Profonde était la nécessité du meurtre bienfaisant,
du meurtre vraiment créateur."

"Comme un homme qui a possédé une femme, la
femme disparaît pour un moment de sa chair, ainsi
la chose taurine cessait d'être pour lui une obsession,
maintenant qu'il l'avait un peu expurgée en tuant."[1]

As a consequence of the equation woman‹bull, all
the sensations caused by a woman in her lover, can
be awakened by the bull in the taurophile, chiefly
sensations of a sadic and coprophilic nature:

"He adored bulls, as we know, but his cult of this
particular bull had grown all the more quickly

[1] These passages are amusingly bowdlerised in the English
version. Take for instance the second one: "Once a man has
had his desire, for a time he is free from the very thought of it;
now that he had killed something beside beef cattle in the
slaughter‹house, the thought of bulls ceased to be an obsession."

79

because he was afraid of him, and because he hoped that his worship might mitigate his wrath: 'Dirty beast! Pig! Swine!'"

And in the same way as he, in the aura of female odour, had snuffed *l'âcre ferment qui sort des choses contaminées*, so he wallows now in the *odeur excitante du crottin* of the symbolical beast.[1]

Successively, the bull becomes his dominant thought, and all things put on a taurine appearance to the eyes of the obsessed person:

"If the train passed a herd of cows, his fellow-travellers were astonished to see Alban spring to his feet as if galvanised, and dash to the corridor where he devoured the dreary cattle [2] with eyes bulging from his forehead."

He spends his days stretched out on the bed (i.e. on the bull), devouring a glossary of bull-fighting. He collects old Greek coins of Marseilles, because some show a bull's horn, others a bull walking, and still others a bull charging. He uses those coins instead of buttons for his clothes. He finds that bulls are recalled by crocodiles, and, also, by street cars. (No wonder, since Ramón Gómez de la Serna com-

---

[1] The English translation is very tame: "the *evil* ferment of contaminated things" for the former, "the *strong* smell of the *stable*" for the latter passage.

[2] *Le bétail morne.* Mr. Rich has: "the sad-eyed beasts"!

pares a bull to a tall motor-cycle without rider, *una alta motocicleta sin jinete*, and even to a stormy gun charging with fixed bayonet, *un borrascoso cañón que cargase a la bayoneta.*) The dashes of red marking the olive-trees display the same bright red of the *intérieur du cheval ouvert.* (Curiously enough, Montherlant had just declared: "I can't even imagine what hanging entrails look like," to show that the attention of the real *aficionado* is never fastened upon that unsavoury part of the spectacle.) All other feelings pale by the side of tauromania: "Why, the most inspired masterpiece on canvas is a pale sort of thing compared with a bull glaring at you with nothing between you and him!" (Gautier had already said: "*Cette situation vaut tous les drames de Shakespeare.*")

From labouring under such an obsession to investing this taurine omnipresence with an actual religious character there is but a short step, and nobody could perform it with more nimbleness than Henri de Montherlant, a fervent Catholic, as he is pleased to proclaim himself emphatically. On this Catholicism of his the author had dwelt with some length in a previous volume, *Le Songe*, where, among the most exquisitely Catholic acts, he includes fornication and the refreshing experience of killing an enemy. A *quid divinum* is recognised in this latter experience also by no less an independent authority than D. H. Lawrence (*Kangaroo*):

"(Jack Calcott) reached his face towards Somers with weird, gruesome exultation, and continued in a hoarse, secret voice:—Cripes, there is nothing bucks you up like killing a man—nothing. You feel a perfect angel after it."

After this, there can be few doubts left about the orthodoxy of an act comparatively so much milder as that slaughtering of cattle, no matter how elabo/ rate, which is a bull/fight. If not actually in the Bible or the Holy Fathers, we shall find abundant evidence of the deep Catholicity of bull/fights in the constant tradition of the most Catholic of nations, Spain: *El arte de los toros bajó del cielo.* . . . Ayala quotes the doggerel of the popular *zarzuelita* not without a smile. But Montherlant is in dead earnest.

All over Spain, no canonisation ceremony, no transference of the Blessed Sacrament or of relics to a new church, ever took place, nor any celebration in honour of a patron Saint, without a bull/fight in connection with it. Ecclesiastical chapters and bishops vied with each other in instituting bull/fights at their own expense, and the Dean of the Chapter of Burgos himself actually wrote and published a *Tauromachia.* The canonisation of a single saint, Saint Teresa, cost the lives of more than two hundred bulls, for every one of the convents of her founda/

BULL-FIGHT IN PIAZZA SAN PIETRO IN ROME DURING THE
JUBILEE OF 1500

82]

tion organised a fight. No wonder, since the Holy
Ghost, through the medium of Pope Borgia, who
had the bull in his crest, had confirmed the sanctity
of tauromachias on the occasion of the Jubilee of
1500 at Rome, when a super-corrida took place in the
square before St. Peter's. Nothing is left to us but to
bow before this and similar evidence produced by
our learned taurophile. Even if one is impious
enough to hesitate before some of the authorities
adduced, Pope Alexander the Sixth's approval really
hits the bull's eye. That approval affords the best
guarantee of Christianity for the taurine sacrament.
Besides, who can resist the arguments of a French
writer in the humour for Catholicism? Whatever
you do, he is sure to take the bull by the horns.
While we wait for a papal bull (has Montherlant
ever meditated over the mystical concordance implied by this English word?), the bull of a new Pope
Borgia, to dedicate to this cult the bull-breeding
stud-farms, let us be content with watching
Henri de Montherlant turning the bull-rings into
churches, and visiting them in a sort of religious
pilgrimage, since he finds there the sublimest com-
forts of Faith. The toreros are the priests of those
mystical slaughter-houses:

"Their dress capes heavy with gold braid, and
their expressions, made one think of a group of

priests and acolytes waiting in the sacristy for the procession to the altar to begin."

The bull and the torero fighting are the god and his priest *"qui édifient leur communion prochaine et la murent dans une danse nuptiale."*

"In the silence, the bell of a cabestro rang, as though for Elevation."

And, as everything in the bull-ring reminds Alban de Bricoule of a church, so everything in a church recalls to him the bull-ring. A statue of the Virgin moves him deeply:

"Was it excess of religious fervour that he felt? Or was it because the teeth showing through the half-open mouth made him think tenderly of his beloved bulls, who have small teeth too? At any rate, he almost broke out into a *saeta* of his own fashioning: 'Ah, how easily I could close that mouth of yours!' Naturally he was not thinking of doing so by argument. Perhaps the idea was a trifle coarse, but there was no malice in it, and he quickly realised that it went beyond the pale. Then he felt that he loved the Virgin all the more for having insulted her. . . . What a happy disposition!"

"Quelle heureuse nature!" No doubt the breast of

Our Lady of Sorrows pierced with seven swords must remind Alban de Bricoule of "the young bulls who, pierced with swords and about to die, flee before the amateur matador." A happy disposition indeed, for which bull-slaughtering is not a sort of refined butchery, but rather *une incantation religieuse*.

But, after all, even the presentation of bull-fights in terms of Catholicism is perhaps a thing too obvious and commonplace. Some exotic spice is needed to make the dainty still more toothsome. This exotic spice is aptly supplied by Mithraism, a religion apropos of which Alban, at times, *"allant jusqu'au bout de son obscure génie"* "felt moved to make a revival of it his mission":

"In spite of himself Mithra slew the Bull, but from his blood came wine, from his marrow, corn and every plant that grows, and from his seed, every animal useful to man. The deed of blood brought forth all the good things of earth, and the Bull's horn became the symbol of plenty. And, when the world came to an end, Mithra would come again to sacrifice the Bull in his divinity. But out of the second sacrifice would come not an earthly life, but the resurrection of the body and the soul, with eternal punishment and reward."

Alban de Bricoule, *alias* Viscount Henri de Montherlant, is going to be the new Mithra, the new Messiah:

"Theywent downtoexaminethe ring. The great bulk of the church overhung it, quite close and with all its height, as though the plaza and the church had been all of a piece. Even so in the arena at Nîmes a steeple, and in the arena at Arles a statue of Our Lady, towers above the enclosure. And Alban, who liked spiritual peace, felt once more filled with a tranquil joy at this fresh testimony to the recon-ciliation of Mithra with Christ."

As the result of a daring syncretism, Mithra and Christ are reconciled, made identical. But Henri de Montherlant is the new Mithra, and, needless to say, the new Christ. *Quelle heureuse nature!* Once sin-ners used to expiate in bitterness of soul all their sins, before turning into saints; to-day, in the century of speed, even sinners have become quicker, and, in order to be canonised, they need only proclaim the profound holiness of their sins. O, happy, happy dispositions!

A happy disposition for a religious man is shown by this Montherlant, if not actually for a bull-fighter. When he faces the bull, he feels himself *"soulevé de terre comme les mystiques par un extraordi-naire bonheur corporel et spirituel,"* he feels he is living *"une de ces hautes minutes délivrées où nous apparaît quelque chose d'accompli, que nous tirons de nous-mêmes et que nous baptisons Dieu."* But, in the capa-city of bull-fighter, he belongs to the *tueurs aux nerfs de femme*, and, frankly, many of the gestures of that rite he celebrates in front of the bull re-semble, *à s'y méprendre*, not so much the gestures of a priest, as, rather, those of a man overcome with fear. No wonder, since Alban de Bricoule had taken to bull-fighting as a treatment for a nervous breakdown! As one sees, Huysmans of *A rebours* has still a following.

There is a country to which sexually obsessed intellectuals are sure to turn sooner or later. Davos is the final stage for consumptives; the Davos of the sexually obsessed intellectuals is Spain. When Friedrich Nietzsche lost his balance, he exalted the music of *Carmen*; precociously dilapidated Pierre Louÿs, the precious calligrapher, sought for stimu-lants in the land of Conchita; Albert Samain, sapped by consumption, compared his soul to *une Infante en robe de parade*; Maurice Barrès, a fervent Catholic of the class of Viscount de Montherlant, rubbed his exasperated senses against the thorns of Spanish mys-ticism. More recently, Anglo-Saxon authors have complicated the exotic appeal by transferring the scene from Spain to colonial Spain, chiefly Mexico, and by adding to the time-hallowed spices the wild drumming and abdominal mysticism of the Indians: some of them go so far as to wish that the Japanese would conquer Mexico, so as to make the exotic pot-pourri all the more irresistible.

According to Barrès, the pleasures of the bull-fight and the auto-da-fé, when they reach the plane of intellect, result in asceticism. The aisles of the churches are nothing else but alcoves, deep alcoves, where beings made for *collaborer à des sensibilités raffinées*, covered with long dark veils, whisper in the confessionals their sins, their passionate sins. Spanish churches are full of that smell of decay which is cal-culated to send the voluptuous *blasé* to the seventh heaven. From behind the *reja, "précieuse au toucher comme un beau corps de femme,"* he adores *"ces poupées faisandées, ces corps déshabillés et saignants, ces genoux et ces coudes écorchés du Christ."* Christ is imagined as a martyr youth, rubbed by women with precious spices and balsams. Like St. Sebastian in D'Annunzio's drama: *"Toi, toi, bel Archer, toi, si beau!"* Finikin Barrès, while travelling in Spain, *"ne laissait aucune occasion d'être froissé."* An expert taster of women's tears, he skilfully selects Toledo as an ideal sojourn for Bérénice:

"If the dourness of Toledo were not sufficient to oppress Bérénice and make her touching for us, as much as it is necessary, there is a last stroke by which

we would know how to afflict her: in that sun-
parched and sun-baked town, where the smell of
benzoin coming from the rocks merges in the smell
of candles issuing from the immense cathedral, we
would show the child tormented with hunger."

And, in case Bérénice's tears were not deemed
touching enough, Barrès will remember that "*des
âmes subtiles se lèvent du sang versé, une vapeur nous
pénètre et réveille en nous la bête carnassière.*"

"La volupté et la mort, une amante, un squelette,
sont les seules ressources sérieuses pour secouer
notre pauvre machine."

Now when the *bête carnassière*, the beast of prey,
is a being made of bones, muscles, and blood, un-
mistakably built for a violent physical life, so pre-
disposed by God to attack and rape, as Blake's Tiger
"burning bright in the forests of the Night," a not
impossible brother to the mild Lamb, in the in-
scrutable mystery of Creation, then that beast of
prey may be thought ferocious and formidable, but
nevertheless, admirable on account of the perfect
adequacy of his life to his energy. So admirable
indeed, that the brave man, the accomplished
warrior, is compared with him. But the calculated
ferocity of the sexually obsessed intellectual is not

the ferocity of the tiger, but, rather, that of an animal *du type écureuil*, that type Barrès ascribes to El Greco: *"cet homme tout de finesse, de nervosité, la tête légèrement inclinée à gauche, du type écureuil, si j'ose dire, mais ennobli de rêverie religieuse."* This little feline creature does not know how to tear to pieces and devour, but he can manage a lick and a bite; best of all he likes carrion, *faisandé* flesh, diseased bodies, hospital veterans, candidates for the nursing home. His morbid attraction for tormented and crucified bodies is pompously labelled by him: Catholicism. His sexual *Katzenjammer* is termed by him: Art. His hysteria of emotional poses over the body of the fallen enemy, his lachrymose obsession for the burials of his own dead (he would almost like to cut the enemy's throat on the gaping grave, as in the times of Troy), are the chief ingredients of his love for his own country. Like Kleist's Penthesilea, this little beast of prey loves what he kills, and kills what he loves: a *tueur aux nerfs de femme*. The tiger is cruel and noble, but the *type écureuil* just described is cruel and, to say it in good Castilian, *asqueroso*.

One feels rather sorry that Maurice Barrès should have chosen as the exponent of his hispano-sadistic fits that odd and mannered genius, Doménicos Theotocópoulos called El Greco. The question of El Greco's art was complex enough by itself, even before this further pollution at the hands of Barrès's slimy sensuality. *Nihil quod tetigit non in* *quinavit*. But, like the Old Man of the Mountain in the Arabian tale, the little *bête carnassière* sits on the neck of the quaint painter to the point of stifling him with the sophisms of his interpretation. While once one felt inclined to see in El Greco a mad Tintoretto, after Barrès's book it has become the fashion to see the ill-fated painter in the terms of a colourist Barrès, and to proclaim as his masterpieces the *Immaculate Conception* in the Church of San Vicente, Toledo, and the *Descent of the Holy Ghost* in the Prado, those being the most mannered among his compositions, those which answer best to Barrès's formula. In El Greco's art, the French artist warns us, those paintings represent what the *Second Faust* is in Goethe's, the *Vie de Rancé* in Chateaubriand's, the last verse in Hugo's work:

"I do love those mysterious works of the great artists grown old. . . . Eager to express themselves, disdaining to explain their meaning, contracting their means of expression as they have shortened their sign manual, they achieve weight, they attain to the concision of enigmas and epitaphs. Do their nearly worn out senses put them apart from, and leave them on the outskirts of, the universe? They appear to us detached from all externals, lonely in

91

the midst of their experiences which they turn into lyric wisdom.''

There is no perfection outside precocity and senility, for the refined author. The healthy ripe-ness of life does not interest him. Because healthy ripeness is serene, but unripe adolescence and soft senility are tormented ages, and therefore so much more interesting from a sadistic point of view. How interesting is the painter enfeebled in his inspiration as well as in his eyesight, who repeats his old dodges with the haziness of negatives out of focus; since for Barrès this is not an effect of decaying power, but of elaboration of the same ideas, ''always the same and every time instinct with more meaning'': meta-physical painting! How interesting is the so-called Daughter of El Greco, "*cette émouvante fiévreuse*" with beautiful eyes, a pure oval face, and olive com-plexion, adored by æsthetes and decadents, one who never had actual existence outside their *imagination excitée*! In that lady Barrès saw the painter's model for the Virgin: ''his daughter whom he deifies every day better.'' (Did Barrès imply a sort of incest complex, I wonder?)

If, at least, all this had the merit of novelty! Whereas it is only an adaptation to Spanish things of the mystico-sensual rhetoric which the Pre-Raphaelites, Walter Pater, and J. A. Symonds, had worked out for the Italian Renaissance. "Second-hand vice, sure, of all is the most nauseous."

If, at least, Barrès had said the last word! But the formula of mystic and sombre Spain—blood, lust, death—is still being retailed by provincial scribblers, spread with the mechanical persistency of popular tunes, welcomed with enthusiasm by the audiences of picture-houses.

Curiosity and prepossession—as Magalotti remarks—cause one to fail to pay attention to the flavour of a thing; rather, the soul, fond of it by hearsay, goes forward to meet it, and, before the quality of the flavour in its natural state reaches her, she sprinkles it from the distance with the imagined sweetness of which she has the source in herself; so that, when she finally approaches it, she feels it such as she has made it, not such as it actually is; and, while enjoying her own essence under the appearance of the thing, she believes she is enjoying the thing itself.

The gory, furious, bull; the scourged, patient, Christ; Don José Navarro betrayed and raging; Don Mateo Diaz bamboozled and submissive; the dagger in the heart of Our Lady of Pain; the stiletto in the heart of Carmen: it is always the same joint hanging from different hooks, in the romantic Spanish shambles. Spanish cookery, solid and monotonous. Blood and lust for lunch, blood and death for dinner. Always with a dash of mysticism, since "wherever your skill fails, do not spare black shadows," as a painter said to his young disciple.

It was from the window of the train which drove us to Valladolid that in the distance, along the railway-line, we descried a patch of a very bright red. This patch made a pretty sight, set off as it was by the burnt-ochre background of the barren earth, under a spotless cobalt sky. Like a poppy amidst corn, like a carnation against a tawny cheek, the scarlet patch allured our eye and, refusing to be identified with a precise form, kept our judgment suspended in an alternative of pleasant hypotheses. But as soon as the train came nearer, we saw the men bent over that bright red, and presently that red revealed itself as the bare carcass of an old flayed horse. The peasants were flaying it with the curved knives, methodically, close by the railway-line. The burnt-red of the clots of blood, the purple of the muscles, the wax yellow of the sinews, all the pitiable undress of the slaughtered animal flashed before our eyes for a moment. And the men who tore the skin with a noise of rustling silk. It was the carcass of a dead horse. A miserable gory carrion: nothing else.

Behind the high-falutin' descant of Barrès, Montherlant & Co.—blood, lust, death—you will not find much else.

THE ALHAMBRA
AND CHURRIGUERRA

THE ALHAMBRA
AND CHURRIGUERRA

Mais Grenade a l'Alhambra—V. Hugo

READER, I did not take up my abode between the
magic walls of the Alhambra for four days and as
many nights, with the tacit consent of the authori‹
ties, neither did I dwell there for several months,
attended by houris and escorted by valets descended
from the Moorish kings. I did not loiter about the
fairy courts and halls, in the friendly silences of the
moonlight, nor linger in the deep alcoves, to dream
of beautiful odalisques leaning on voluptuous
pillows, drowsed with the perfumes of the balmy
climate and with the accents of a music sweet.
While I looked down from the balconies upon
chivalric Granada, I did not hear a faint nocturnal
sound of castanets rise from the gardens of the
Darro, or the quivering pizzicato of a guitar accom‹
pany a passionate voice soaring from some solitary
lane; neither did I succeed in seeing the white arm
of some mysterious princess beckon from a gallery,
or some dark eye sparkle through the lattice. The
sultana Chain‹of‹hearts and the Moor Tarfe in his
white burnous appeared to me only in the deplor‹
able photographs which are offered to a tourist in

G   97

quest of picturesque materialisations. None of the bits of luck which fell to the lot of Washington Irving and Théophile Gautier was repeated for me. My mind was not haunted by any of the many delicious follies, pleasant whimwhams, and gentle absurdities that the tearful Edmondo De Amicis claims to have thought and uttered between the Court of the Myrtles and the Court of the Lions. While visiting the Alhambra I did not tremble like an aspen leaf; while leaving it I did not bid farewell to all the illusions of youth and to that love which will never live again. I did not regret that all those who are dear to me were not present at the fascinating spectacle, so that I might take a snapshot of them disposed in a group, with the picturesque fountain in the background. Finally—I must confess it, at the cost of losing my reputation in your eyes, reader—I did not let myself be photographed, alone at least, in that sublimest of photographer's studios. This unique opportunity for watering at the eyes, trembling like a leaf, saying sweet nonsense to imaginary sultanas, and being photographed in a supremely picturesque setting, I let it slip for ever, alas and welladay!

From the bottom of my soul I deplore the inauspicious influence of stars which did not predispose my imagination to conceive a *guía emocional* of the Alhambra on the lines of the one by the sensitive

ALHAMBRA

Patio de la Reja

Martínez Sierra. Even if I were a millionaire, nothing would induce me to build a duplicate of the Court of the Lions in my park, as the picturesque Théo dreamed; I leave such whims to the proprietors of *tabarins*, night-clubs, and similar institutions *de luxe*. But, while I was looking at those arabesques, those honeycombed cupolas, those fabulous halls, I was again overwhelmed by a sense of monotony. Perhaps I have not got the key which might unlock for me the secret of this delicate art. What are the Arabs to me? It is all very well to tell me that the eleventh-century Arabs thought the European races unfitted for the cultivation of the sciences and arts, that in their multitude of supernatural visions they anticipated Dante, in their love-lyrics the "sweet new style," in their architecture the Renaissance Florentines. For a moment, in the Court of the Reja or in that of Daraxa I can conjure up the image of a quiet Tuscan cloister; and the slenderness of the columns, the sobriety of the entablatures, the sombre fragrance of the cypresses, the intermittent murmur of the fountains, the glimpses of hilly country through the bays (a country pale with olive-trees, interspersed with dark notes of cypresses)—all this delicate and severe grace has the power of reviving in me the memory of some timeless hour spent at Poggio Gherardo, at Settignano, or who knows where and when, in Tuscany, an hour so different and still of the same flavour. I seem to become aware of some mysterious relation such as might cause a man, on hearing the cock-crow, to think of a dove's cooing tuned an octave higher. On entering the Court of the Myrtles, or looking at the *acequia* of the Generalife, the phantom of the Pazzi Chapel in Santa Croce of Florence, with a pond in the place of the gravel alley, may loom before my eyes as if by witchcraft; and though the likeness is eventually destined to appear illusory to the eye of reason, still, no doubt, the suggestion of a few analogous *motifs*—slenderness of columns, perhaps, or something more deeply interfused in the bitter fragrance of the sombre foliage and in the very subtlety of the air—is sufficient to create a wistful feeling of anticipation, as in telepathy. At the end of the avenue of sublime cypresses leading to the Generalife I would almost have expected the tragic façade of the Villa dei Collazzi, and, while I was contemplating from the Albaicín the acropolis of the Alhambra, with its cypresses and olive-trees, red against the snowy background of the Sierra Nevada, why should I have been reminded of San Miniato—church, tower, cemetery—clean-cut against the white range of wintry Vallombrosa? Was this feeling of a tantalising affinity a mere play of my imagination which, faced with an alien spectacle, tried to render it more familiar and to understand it by

translating it into a well-known language? Was it
because that world was so distant from me, that I
tried to represent it to my eyes as mysteriously near?
Just as in all the faces of the women whom one man
has loved there seems to be an indefinable family
likeness, a share in the same kind of charm, just so,
perhaps, the courts and gardens of the Zoraydas
and Lindaraxas appeared to me as dream images of
the cloisters and orchards of the Simonettas and
Fiordispinas? Was it this same illusion which caused
me to discover a secret affinity between the paintings in the Hall of Justice and the frescoes of the
Cappellone degli Spagnoli? An illusion, at any rate,
not mine alone, since I read that no less an authority
than Mr. Berenson shared it. By what mysterious
links, then, were Florence and Granada connected
once?

Still, it *is* an illusion. I need only leave the courts
and enter the halls to feel the weight of an alien,
distant world. A world which is complicated only in
appearance; in reality it is intoned on a single note,
like the *Arabian Nights* in which, the more you read
them, the less does the variety of names and events
serve to conceal the fundamental monotony, so that,
in the end, the differences appear too thin to stand
out, and everything seems arrayed in the same plane,
by a two-dimensional technique with fixed formulas
and stereotyped endings. An art without individu-

ality, where the wealth of decoration is calculated to conceal the poverty of the inspiration. An art which is generally attributed to boundless fantasy, whereas it never leaves a groove, and by a multiplication of its elements never succeeds in producing a *tertium quid*, a miracle. All the princes of the Arabian tales are the same prince, all the maidens the same maiden, all the pleasure-gardens the same garden plot, all the magicians the same wizard. There exists the type, refined into as graceful a hieroglyph as you please, but still remaining a type, an abstraction, a formula. After reading the Arabian tales you will not be haunted with a precise memory of person or place, but rather with a vague feeling as of an enchanted limbo where shadows, not shapes, move about, and voices are heard which seem to issue from the air, not from living mouths. And all this world admits of infinite combinations of its elements, like a kaleidoscope made of a few pieces of glass. So light is the weight of the individual, so little personal the succession of events, that the tales seem to telescope into each other, become blurred in our recollection, melt like dreams, without abrupt transitions or unexpected jerks. It is a light goblin world of aerial smoke and iridescent bubbles, a golden elixir with a slight suspicion of an intoxicating drug at the bottom, of a gentle fallacy, whose disclosure would dissolve that world in the twinkling of an eye.

Such is the Alhambra. Walk through its halls, strain your eyes on the arabesques of the walls and the patterns of the glazed tiles, survey the landscape through the elaborately carved windows. It is always the same hall, the same wall, the same window. The artist has impressed the coat of stucco with the same stamp, cunningly alternating the disposition so as to create the illusion of an infinite variety; but, if you look closely, the patterns are few, the colours are few, and monotony prevails. The stalactite cupolas overhang you like sectioned beehives, with a feminine fragility of laces, as if an artichoke-like crinoline with concentric flounces were suspended over your head. More fragile still: they have the frothy lightness of meringues and Malayan swallow's nests: things made of whisked-up white-of-egg, or silk-like saliva. An illusive variety: the same geo-metrical dodge multiplied in a hundred different treatments. Such artifice bids fair to captivate a heedless eye, but is not powerful enough to cheat a diligent inspection. It tires without giving satisfac-tion; it makes one think of a mirror-cased room re-flecting the same feature down infinite corridors of illusion. There is no counterpoint in this music, no third dimension in this painting, this poetry is monorhyme. And not because the material is not noble enough, but because the formula, happy as it may be, repeats itself mechanically, the Alhambra produces that impression of precariousness, as if, at a strong puff of your lips, the honeycombed cupolas should float away like thistledown, and the embroidered walls be rent as easily as cobwebs.

The Alhambra has the perfection of cobwebs, beehives, snow-crystals, frost-flowers on a window pane. It is perfect as only the automatic work of infallible instinct can be perfect. But from cobwebs, beehives, snow-crystals, frost-flowers, genius is absent. None of us would dream of classifying as works of art those sublime natural products. Geometrical regularity is not nearer to order than the life of the bees is to the life of a human collectivity. The bees have no history; the formula of their lives has been discovered and codified for ever. Their perfection is limited and motionless. There is no creative activity in it, no stress and struggle, nothing unforeseen. Perhaps this is the reason why Arab civilisation was destined to fade away almost without leaving a trace, and the barbarian Europeans rule to-day over the descendants of the Caliphs. Like the Irish art of illumination, Arab art was born perfect, and crystallised. This impersonal perfection, multiplied to the point of monotony, is a characteristic of the East. Can a European eye be content with those colossal aggregations of similar sculptures that are the Indian temples? Can it be satisfied with the multiplane roofs of the pagodas? Oriental art obeys

such principles as control the casts of earth-
worms; it proceeds by super-imposition. Or, rather,
it does not proceed: it echoes its own formula an infinite number of times. European art, on the contrary, is development. The relation of Asiatic to
European art is not unlike that of the insect to the
mammal world. With a few patterns cunningly
handled you can reconstruct an Alhambra, but you
cannot reproduce the frieze of the Parthenon, nor
one of the portals of Chartres Cathedral, nor
Giotto's tower, nor Ghiberti's gates. By repeating a
number of times the same group of columns you can
reconstruct the Cordoba mosque, but not a Greek
temple. I think the Arabs had little merit in tying
themselves down to the Mahommedan prohibition
of portraying human features. Had their genius
been really plastic, instead of decorative, the prohibition would have remained a dead letter. Consider
how the Italian taste for polychromy succeeded in
its rebellion against the rigid black and white canon
prescribed by the Counter-Reformation for religious
architecture! The Church of the Gesù, in Rome,
born as bare and drab as a Protestant temple, was
soon lined with precious marbles and decorated with
cheerful paintings. It was ecclesiastical authority,
and not artistic inspiration, which had to bow its
head. But the Arab mind, abstract, mathematical,
was content with multiplying decorative devices.

And once the wheels of the perfect mechanism became worn, the clock stopped for ever.

Can we talk of Arab architecture? Or is it not better to talk of Arab ornamental style? Since, as for the structural part, it is well known that the Arabs did not invent anything. They hung their plaster tapestries on the frame supplied by Byzantine peri-styles, they gave the Roman arches the shape of a horse-shoe. Nothing more than a slight touch, just as a Parisian milliner knows, with a deft pressure of her fingers, how to give to the brim of a hat the *dernier cri* shape, and possesses an inimitable skill for trimming it with the fashionable ribbon or trifle. A *soupçon* of the East—like a Parisian trade-mark—was what the Arabs contributed; but the structure of the buildings remained the invention of others. In Europe they were usurpers, they did not make good their conquest. But they infused into the Spaniards, together with their blood, their Oriental taste for monotonous decoration, for the art of multiplying without developing, for the *motif* which adorns without creating anything new.

In San Juan de los Reyes of Toledo one finds a Christian translation of the decorative style of the Alhambra. The Christian treatment is compara-tively much heavier, so that no illusion is any longer possible about the quality of the material employed. In that deserted nave, full of the twittering and fluttering of the swallows and sparrows which have their nests in the half-ruined vault, the two pulpits look like clumsy nests made of mud and twigs, and the stuccoes of the walls take the chalky and brittle appearance of the stale excrement of birds. The style is imitated, but the lightness of execution has gone. Neither is there the solidity peculiar to the crowded decorations of Lombard or German style. Fragility without lightness; mud, stucco, dung, friable and perishable, in the forsaken church.

All the decorative modes of the Spaniards are to be traced to the Arab, Oriental tradition. Plate-resque (i.e. silversmith's) style is the happy definition of the kind of taste which dominated Spanish art during two centuries. The skill is concentrated on the working out of details, regardless of structure and line. A goldsmith's art, meticulous, aiming at strange, dazzling effects, reckoning on quantity rather than on quality, simulating richness of invention by sheer accumulation. The detail is not an organic one; it does not answer to a special function, neither is it part of a whole. It is a scroll, a shell, a palmette, an arabesque, a trinket, which might be placed here as well as there, interchangeable, capricious. Even when the executing hand is skilful, the selecting brain is mediocre. It is a provincial art which confuses redundancy with richness, and over-does it. On the other hand, the detail is not always skilfully executed; sometimes the artist behaves like one of those pianists who try to conceal the deficiencies of their performance behind a nimble rapidity of motion apt to deceive only inexperienced ears. And, needless to say, this goldsmith's art is terribly monotonous.

The Renaissance meant for Spain rather a decorative than an architectural style: the plateresque. Baroque meant little else. In Austria and Southern Germany, the influence of Borromini's baroque resulted in the promotion of a school of local talents, which developed originality and reached its climax with the immortal inventions of a Fischer von Erlach, a Hildebrandt, a Prandauer. In Spain, that same influence became crystallised in the decorative manner of Churriguerra. Arab art partook of the charm of illuminated books, plateresque style could vie with goldsmith's work, but Churriguerra's manner is only matched by the virtuosity of a first-rate *chef*.

The altar of Santa Tecla in the Burgos Cathedral, tooled and gilded like a casket, fretted, goffered, scalloped, trimmed with candy-like bunches of artificial flowers—a nick-nack one may hesitate whether to associate with the palate or with the eye—is more like the overcrowded shrines of the Hindu divinities than one would think at first. But the climax of Spanish baroque, a very poor one, if you compare it with San Carlino in Rome, the Zwinger in Dresden, the Nepomukkirche in Munich, and the Belvedere in Vienna, is reached in the Sacristy of the Cartuja in Granada.

In San Clemente el Real of Seville the link with Arab decoration is more evident, because of the fretwork (*artesonado*) ceiling and the glazed tile dados with which the thoroughly frescoed walls are framed. But the Cartuja is still more representative, since there the Arab taste, instead of being deliberately imitated, forms an integral part of the artist's mind. So that in two monuments of Granada, the Alhambra and the Cartuja, one may almost read in epitome the history of Spanish decorative art.

In the Sacristy of the Cartuja costly materials rub shoulders with gesso and scagliola; the cedar presses are inlaid with ivory, motherofpearl, and silver, vying in richness with Arab work; the slabs of rare marbles of the altar are put together with such a consummate skill as the craftsmen who worked in San Martino, in Naples, would not have disdained. But the vaults, pilasters, corbels, the entire cornice, consist of stucco no less snowwhite than a weddingcake. Like a clever pastrycook, Luís de Arévalo has taken pleasure in collecting a great quantity of ingredients for his architectural *puchero*; every dainty thing is to be found in the white sacristy, as in a cookery exhibition. The hall is like a sugar grotto, the costly furniture has the glossy brown colour of crisp almond-cakes, the marbles look like concretions of candied fruits, the walls are scalloped like festoons of whipped cream, the doors ape chocolate cakes. The throne room in Cockaigne could hardly be conceived otherwise. A uniform sugariness, as monotonous as the pleasure-grounds described by Marino. Every corner is crammed with ornament, no inch of wall is left blank; the *motifs* are repeated, multiplied, royal icing is piled on royal icing as in a wedding-cake, laces overlap laces, flounces are set off by more flounces as in a complicated hoop-skirt. We are reminded of the Alhambra.

Why, then, in front of a monument of this kind should one think of elaborate cakes and overtrimmed dresses? Because there is no loftiness of line to organise into a whole the various decorative elements, to raise the onlooker's intellect to the sphere of pure form or pure colour, so that such accidentals as are the quality of the materials and the occasional quaintness of the signs may merge in, and be transcended by, a superior concept. Neither, as it happens in the Church of San Martino in Naples, does the pictorial effect so achieved justify and redeem the lavishness of the means used. Matter remains matter and, as such, invites the mind to wander through the multiplicity of the appearances, while it suggests liminal forms of art: the decorative skill

GRANADA

The Sacristy of the Cartuja

110]

of confectioners and dressmakers. Here the baroque has achieved a parody of its very self, almost as in Basile's *Pentamerone*. A light touch would be enough to transform into a grotesque fancy this indigestible plethora of marble, metal, wood, stucco.

Such as it is, overlaid with ornament, hybrid, amorphous, the Cartuja hangs between the East and the West, the curious temple of a curious town. The pilasters, all a running carving of capitals, are indeed pillars of a Hindu temple; in fact, in a Hindu temple is very likely to be found their prototype, since Ferdinando da Bibbiena, who first introduced such pilasters into his stage-settings, combed all periods and styles for suggestions. They are obtained by the repeated superimposition of the same element, and give the impression of resulting from one of those happy mechanisms of the vegetable world, whereby similar crowns of leaflets shoot and grow together on the same stalk, or from one of those pyrotechnical tricks which cause similar versicolour rockets to hiss out of the core of one single flower-bomb, until the last gleam fades away in the fathomless night.

This kind of decorative invention is essentially Eastern. Since the Eastern mind likes to proceed through concatenations of similar concentric spaces. The East has given us the Chinese boxes, the sets of tables that pack one inside the other, so popular in the eighteenth century, the tales linked together by a frame story, the parallel hierarchies of angels. The Eastern mind tries to convey the idea of the infinite through the repetition of the similar, by an exclusively quantitative, mathematical process. A figure is caused to pass through its multiples, until the mind, having set out upon the infallible progression, gets lost in the infinity of the suggested spiral. But, while the Eastern mind affects the open, inorganic form, the European mind demands the closed, organic form. For the Eastern mind the supernatural becomes identified with all or with nothing; for the European mind the supernatural localises itself, postulates order and co-ordination, a system. For the European mind a column has a plinth, a shaft, a capital, and the architrave rests on the abacus; the whole is instinct with a rhythm that causes this artificial organism to partake of the divine symmetry of the human body.

> Servantes sans genoux,
> Sourires sans figures,
> La belle devant vous
> Se sent les jambes pures.

But the Eastern column may be prolonged to infinity, because there is no relation of parts in it, but only multiplication of the same element. You may imagine the interior of the Sacristy of the Cartuja prolonged in height like a telescope, and the general effect would remain the same. In the same way you

could develop at discretion the walls of the Alhambra, and make the honeycombed ceilings more
elaborate still. What can stop the progression,
since the basis is a mere mathematical series? But if
one tampers with quantities in a Greek or Romanesque or Gothic temple, harmony is destroyed,
since European mind is proportioned measure and
measured proportion. Any addition, at a given
moment, appears superfluous.

Who else but a Spaniard, the architect Gaudí,
was likely to attempt to modernise Gothic architecture by the intrusion of an Oriental principle? In
the Church of the Sagrada Familia, in Barcelona, he
has indulged in a useless profusion of similar
elements, and sacrificed the essential harmony of the
various parts in order to suggest the infinite by degrading to the rank of decorative elements structural
motifs derived from Gothic architecture. In the
Sagrada Familia the window is no longer related to
the neighbouring elements, the open gallery does
not contrast its subdued continuity with the self-
contained circle of the rose; no harmonious, necessary frame can be inferred from the exterior. The
Sagrada Familia is no less arbitrary than the castles
of sand made by children on the shore. Whereas in
a Gothic building a displacement in the position of
the various elements is sufficient to upset the harmony of the whole (let us think of the façade of

Siena Cathedral), in an erection of an Eastern character like Gaudí's one may invert, redouble, suppress, without imperilling the combined result. Infinity suggested by monotony: as during insomnia one keeps repeating a word, a formula, until consciousness is lost. The Alhambra, the Escorial, the Cartuja, the Sagrada Familia, are expressions of the same race.

If European art ever did come near to the art of the East, it was in the baroque period, with its renunciation of design for the sake of colour, of the closed form for the sake of the open form, of structure in favour of decoration.

Like an arabesque, a *concetto* remains isolated in its self-sufficiency. A metaphysical poem resolves itself into a sequence of madrigals, a multitude of decorative puns. The *Raghuvamcha*, the *Megadhuta* seem products of baroque imagination. Du Bartas's *Divine Sepmaine*, Crashaw's *Weeper* might have been conceived by an Oriental. Why does Marino's *Adone* consist of so many cantos and no more, why does every canto contain so many stanzas and no more, why is there an end of the descriptions of enchanted abodes, entertainments, and pleasures? They could well be protracted, without destroying the economy of the poem. Because the poem has no economy to preserve, no beginning, no middle, no end; it unfolds like a snake, and there

BARCELONA

Church of the Sagrada Familia

is no reason whatever why a snake's body should not be prolonged to infinity. But the body of a mammal or of man does not tolerate such a prolongation. If you prolong such a body, the result is a caricature; but no caricature ensues from the prolongation of a snake's body. There is no interior law under which the adventures of an Arabian tale should at a given moment come to a conclusion, in the same way as there is no law which forbids the protraction of the Thousand and One Nights beyond the figure given in the title. On the other hand, the *Divine Comedy* describes a well-defined line, is a necessary, not an arbitrary, contrivance; parallelism and correlation can be easily discovered in every portion of the poem. Microcosm and macrocosm, symbol and act, allegory and word, everything is linked together, rigorously fastened, inalterable. As in a Romanesque or Gothic cathedral. And yet, somebody has tried to see in Dante an imitator of the Arabs! It is like trying to trace the formula of the Chartres Cathedral in the Cordoba mosque. In the ultramundane fancies of the Arabs, whatever coincidences may be found with the Dantesque poem in the selection of retributions and punishments, and even of certain similes, the wildest arbitrariness reigns. Figures and measures have no precise value, but only a symbolic one: they are meant to suggest infinity, not to specify a real definition of space and time. Who would take literally the "*se pasment vint millier*" of the *Chanson de Roland*? In Dante, on the contrary, every detail is endowed with the solidity of the dogmas of the Catholic Church; it claims to be taken literally.

Therefore the *Divine Comedy* is a drama; there-fore there is a dialectical balance in the various parts of the European building, whether of Greek, or Romanesque, or Gothic, or Renaissance style; there-fore European religion is theology, whereas Eastern religion is mysticism. European religion is an acted mystery, Oriental religion a contemplated mystery. In the mass all the stages of desire, union, satisfac-tion, thanksgiving are adumbrated; in the Arab prayer you have the unrestrained surrender to a superior will.

My restless European mind, fond of variety and drama, recoils from the dreamy monotony of the Alhambra and the Cartuja. To the arabesques and embroideries which digress without concluding, it prefers the elastic and sober line, the exact propor-tion; it expects a logical trend in the works of fiction, an end and an aim. I leave to others to picture their own paradise by the sweet murmur of the fountains, with moonlight to boot. As for me, in order to feel near to God, I need a Romanesque cathedral, mas-sive Norman pillars, solid vaults; I want the sun to mark the floor with precise sheets of light, not to peep through the slashes of an Arab stucco as if through foliage. And if music should be there, let it be organ music. My restless European world is farther from nature, more instinct with humanity, than was the Arab's. Probably because I grew up in a country, like Tuscany, which was from the first ordered and permeated by the handiwork of man.

INTERMEZZO

THE MIRACLE OF SEGOVIA
THE TRIUMPH OF DEATH

At this point it has seemed advisable to the author to relieve the reader with a light intermezzo and a spectacular auto-sacramental in the style of Valdés Leal.

THE MIRACLE OF SEGOVIA

Ségovie a l'autel dont on baise les marches—V. Hugo

As for Segovia, things went wrong from the very beginning. When, on coming to Medina del Campo from Salamanca, I wanted to transform into actual kilometres the potential ones of my yellow Kilomé‹ trico, I was told that the Madrid train via Segovia was one of *composición limitada*, so that I had to wait until they would phone from the preceding station whether there were any seats still available. *"Mas tarde,"* muttered the railway employee, slamming down the slide. I looked around: I was in a squalid station hall, faced with the prospect of having to sleep in one of the beds offered on the first floor (*"Medina del Campo, 2370 ft., Rail. Restaurant, with rooms"*—runs Baedeker: alas, a 2370 feet altitude is not irreconcilable in Spain with what Joly called *"ords lictz tout grenouillans de punaises"* . . . and whenever Baedeker does not comment, something unpleasant lurks behind!) To cheer me up, I had the wail of a beggar whose legs were curled up in a wheeled box, and that beggar was—*tuerto*! A very uneasy half‹hour was spent in conjuring away the evil eye and resisting gloomy forebodings. These

121

latter were by no means dispelled, after I had squeezed myself into a seat of a sort, in the Madrid train.

The corridor was crammed with bags and hat boxes pasted all over with conspicuous hotel labels. The compartments swarmed with English tourists of either sex, whose faces betrayed at a first glance a bond of unanimity. As bees cluster round their queen, so these travellers were bound by invisible strings to a pompous gentleman who was that same worthy heralded by the labels on the baggage and windows: MR. THOMAS'S PARTY. No merciful glance was that cast by the bees on me, an intruder in their hive, but the queen considered with amused pity the isolated tourist, unprotected against the worries of the perilous pilgrimage. Little by little the diffident glances increased my apprehension beyond bearing. What if all these people were going to Segovia? What if they were putting up at the hotel where I had omitted to book my room in advance? Though pompous, Mr. Thomas knew how to relax, occasionally, into a mood of wistful amiability. Now, for example, he was bestowing poetical adjectives on the sunset from the observation platform at the end of the carriage, and thrilling his party by the disclosure that of all the sunsets he had had the privilege of observing in his much-travelled life, this was the best—positively. One of the spinsters took this down in her note-book; others were ecstatically gaping; an albino gentleman peered long at the window through spectacles, till he ejaculated at last: "Oh, I see, the sun—set!"

I felt a little safer once I was inside the *coche* of the Hotel del Comercio y Europeo. Apparently I was the only claimant to the beds of that hostelry. But was this really such a good piece of news? Why, if I were the only one of all those travellers to put up at that hotel, very likely the beds had occupants of another description! Meanwhile, what was to prevent the carriage from starting? Were we waiting for another train? I was watching the English party lining up for two huge motor-buses illuminated as for a pageant. Mr. Thomas, tub-chested, authoritative as a field-marshal, conducted in a quasi-Spanish jargon the work of the burdened porters who heaped pyramids of bags on the top of the buses. But, on my side, what a sad picture it was! Smelly natives were crowding into the capacious carriage in whose sombre recesses I was entertaining faint hopes of board and lodging. As usual, the hotel coach served also as a public bus. And how long the journey proved this time! The two splendid motor-buses were already a good way up the hill; presently they were heard exultantly hooting as they disappeared from our sight, and all this time the sombre coach was groping its way amidst the clouds of dust in their

123

wake. And how it bumped and how it wobbled, and how it rolled, and how it pitched! At every turn of the wheels the passengers were shaken so roughly, that if you shut your eyes you could believe yourself in the belly of Jonah's whale! The women wailed: *"¡Jesumaria!"*—at an occasional lamp/light they could be seen crossing themselves. The men were trying to take the experience playfully, but, at the bends of the road, they leaned against those who sat opposite, and tightened their lips. Every now and then the coach would stop with a bump, and some/body would creep out onto firm ground, stretch his legs, and pay the driver. That journey seemed likely to last until doomsday. At Palencia, at León, at Salamanca, the coach had shown much more sense, and after some ten minutes of switchback over the cobblestones had dropped us at the longed/for ter/minus. This *coche*, however, was more implacable than the famous carriage in *Madame Bovary*; would it rattle us round and round Segovia walls for hours on end, until it broke our backbones and twisted our vitals into Gordian knots? Now a huge devil's bridge arched over our heads, now the ground seemed to give way under us, in a section of road under repair. At last, the centre of the town! The last fellow/passengers got down, and I was alone, again. But what time were we supposed to reach the hotel?—I ventured to ask the driver. He, too, had a

glance of amused pity for me. Was this not the car‚
riage of the Hotel del Comercio y Europeo? Of
course it was: we would be at the hotel in no time.
Despacio.

That journey had taken the best part of an hour.
For a moment I thought I was dreaming a bad
dream, though awake. Because the people I saw
through the windows of the hotel, feeding very
quietly at the tables in the dining‚room, who else
were they, if not Mr. Thomas's party? Oh, they felt
at home! Of course Mr. Thomas had booked the
rooms with at least two months' notice, and the hotel
was as full as an egg. *"Lo siento mucho"*—declared
the señorita: she had no room left for the unfortu‚
nate isolated tourist. May it be that hunger and
despair combined to give a tragic glamour to my
face and a touching eloquence to my tongue? For
when the señorita, after the first off‚hand reply,
deigned to raise her eyes and consider me as a
human being and not as an application for a room,
she softened and promised to do her best; mean‚
while would I go to the dining‚room and have my
meal served? Thank God! This Spanish woman
was hardly endowed with a single dram of *salero*, she
was not particularly attractive, still, in that moment,
I would have exchanged all the virgins of Yemen
(those who "when they love, they die," as the legend
goes) for a single compassionate landlady. Owing to

her, at last, by 11 p.m. I could batten on what Mr.
Thomas's bees had left: it was not much, I must say.
After all this, you would hardly expect me to have
felt very pro-British, that night. Still, before with-
drawing to the wee room (it was the *camarero's* own)
the señorita had saved for the poor non-incorporated
tourist, I was granted by a just God a quarter of an
hour of sweet revenge. It was no dream: that sup-
pliant entreating the señorita was actually Mr.
Thomas who in a cosmopolitan language tried to
explain his lamentable plight: *"Fijese usted madame,
yo ne penso pas dormir in the open air, j'ai droit à une
chambre, usted preparar cama conmigo, bed, lit, anywhere, in the cuarto de baño, prego."* The señorita
held spread under his eyes the letter in which was
stated the number of rooms booked; now the hotel
had not a single room to spare, so the caballero must
needs put up elsewhere for the night, at the Madrileña, of course. Incredible as it may sound, Mr.
Thomas had booked rooms for all the members of
his party, but, somehow, had forgotten to reserve
one for himself. Could he honestly ask one of his
party to share a room with him? Of course not, it
was not done; and there he was, the infallible Mr.
Thomas, entreating for a room like the least provi-
dent of tramps. Wheedling manners, assertive manners, nothing would avail; neither did a *doux sourire
amoureux et souffrant* sit well on those lips lifted en-

126

gagingly on gold and green teeth. So off he went,
led by a sombre porter, towards the mysterious
Madrileña (I did not know, then, that this was the
name of a *fonda*; I rather imagined behind that name
one of Goya's female bugbears). Off he went, ac‹
companied by my wish: "That in your bed you may
find such companions as to cause you to get up to‹
morrow 'without having a place on the whole of
your body, face, and hands, left clear for another
sting,' as one reads in *Guzman de Alfarache!*"

From such companions my bed, contrary to all
expectation, was apparently exempt. The room was
no bigger than a monk's cell; a rickety chair and a
rusty nail were all on which I had to hang my clothes.
When in bed, my hair was winnowed by the draught
which a high skylight let through liberally. The
cracked water jug broke the silence with a plaintive
drip‹drop music. During the night, I dreamed I was
undergoing a torture of which I had read some‹
where, in distant days of boyhood: I was tied to a
column, head and body, and a merciless drop of
water was hitting my skull always in the same place
—it was maddening. At last I gathered enough
strength to put my hand to my head; the feeling of
wetness woke me up completely. Through the sky‹
light it was raining on my hair. This was not the
only adventure of that accursed night. Positively
the squinting beggar of Medina del Campo had cast

a spell on me. At dawn I woke again with a jerk: someone was rummaging next to my bedstead. I saw him bent over the pedestal drawer, in the faint rainy light. "*¿Que quiere usted?*"—a voice rose out of me, almost an alien voice. "*El bolsillo, el mi bol-sillo, caballero.*" Was my purse or my life at stake? Had I fallen into a brigand's den, as in the times of Gil Blas? Such was not the case. The waiter, whose room I was occupying, had simply forgotten his wallet in the drawer, the night before.

As I have said, things went wrong from the very beginning, at Segovia. What happened to me in the evening and during the night, after all, falls under the usual heading of travelling misadventures. But what happened to me on the following day is, I sur-mise, absolutely unprecedented.

In Segovia the present writer was guilty of sacri-lege. Had I done it on purpose, my action might be construed as either an atheist's challenge, or a deca-dent's extravagance. In fact, the catastrophe was brought about by an unheard-of combination of my love of art and the wickedness of a Spanish nail.

What, at the present date, is probably recorded in the capitular archives of the Segovia Cathedral as the Passion Sunday Miracle, I am sorry to say, was in no way contrived by a supernatural agency. Like many other miracles—but let us abstain from blas-phemy, and stick to this particular case.

In the fifth chapel of the left side aisle of Segovia
Cathedral, which is called after Nuestra Señora de la
Piedad, there is a Descent from the Cross, a work of
that rather unsatisfactory disciple of Michelangelo,
Juan de Juní. To say that I was impelled by sheer
love of art to desire acquaintance with that hysterical
sculpture, seems to beg the question, since the
artistic value of that sculpture is very debatable indeed. Perhaps it was the Evil One who, by the spell
of the squinting beggar, lodged that perverse curiosity in my soul. It so happened that, upon entering
the cathedral through the north transept door, I
found that high mass had proceeded as far as the
Prefatio. I glanced at two foreign ladies (one of them
apparently English) sitting in front of the choir *reja*,
to enjoy the spectacle of the service, and, without
any further delay, I turned to the right towards the
chapel of Nuestra Señora de la Piedad. There was
no one in the aisle; the congregation had gathered
on the other side of the choir, and could not be seen
from where I stood. The chapel was there and there
the altar, but, alas, the sculpture above it was
hidden behind a curtain, as usual during the two
weeks before Easter. I have drawn so many curtains
from before altar-pieces, in my sight-seeings, that to
draw one more could not send me to a lower Hell, in
the desperate hypothesis that whoever removes a veil
from before a work of art considered as such and not

I   129

as an object of cult (a case of Jesuitical reservation, as you see) commits a mortal sin. Besides, in Santo Domingo el Antiguo in Toledo, with one paltry peseta I succeeded in silencing a similar religious scruple in a very devout lay sister, and caused her to unveil no less than three paintings; had the sin been a mortal one, it stands to reason that the lay sister would have claimed at least one duro, what do you think?

However this particular curtain proved different from all others. I had no sooner began to furl it, than it warned me by its weight, as if wanting to let me know: "Take heed, I have a difficult temper!" My word, it was as heavy as a stage curtain. I watched it slowly rising: surely it had a heart of iron. When I saw that it was all nicely gathered up at the top, I wound the rope three, four, five times round a nail in the wall, had hardly time to get a glimpse of the tormented Christ, the convulsed Madonna, the by-standers draped in cloaks as hard as battered tin (an excellent illustration of Mr. W. J. Turner's line: "Hysteria calmed into stone")—there was a rush-ing noise as of a pulley, then the altar became like the mouth of a volcano. I was almost caught in a shower of rubble, while clouds of dust drew a veil over the prodigy. An immense thunder rolled along the aisles, echoed in the distant vaults, filled every corner, deafening. The vicious curtain had collapsed on the altar pulling with itself a piece of the wall.

I must own to being not very calm, but I may add that in emergencies I am endowed with more pluck than I should reasonably expect. As if prompted by instinct, I did the only sensible thing. I did not remain as still as a stone, nor did I betake myself to flight. I edged away from the chapel, and with a gait I strived to render as unruffled as possible, with an assumed air of absent-mindedness and contemplation, I sauntered gingerly along the aisle towards the far exit. I kept my eyes fixed on the architectural details of the ceiling and pretended to ignore the breathless acolytes who burst from all the doors of the choir, bewildered, terrified. They passed me by without taking notice, attracted only by the source of the thunder; they flapped their arms like hens upset by the hoot of a motor-car. While the deafening rumble of the prodigy was dying away, the organ had been silenced suddenly, the jubilation of the Sanctus had stopped short, and behind my back there was a stamping of feet, a rustling of cassocks, a banging of doors, an immense hum of excitement—in a word, such a stampede as caused my spine to feel as fidgety as a tickled earwig. I did not turn round. My whole soul was now concentrated on the bottom door of the aisle: would it be open? It was open, there was a bar of light beneath the baize door. I was out; the precincts were deserted, a street sloped down, also deserted. I entered it, running. I looked back. Nobody, there was nobody. Maybe a benignant godhead protected me: was it Pallas Athene who, compassionate to her devotees, threw round me a screen of mist as she did round Ulysses, so that nobody, absolutely nobody could see me walking out of the chapel and leaving the church? In truth, somebody saw me, but, by a rare piece of luck, could not communicate with the others. It was from this one that I learned the sequel, as I shall relate.

Certainly there is within me a potential criminal —and also within you, and within you, too, *"ô hypo crite lecteur, mon semblable, mon frère"*—since as I was speeding along, even before the beating of my heart had subsided, I determined upon creating an alibi. It occurred to me that El Parral must not be very far. *"Oiga, mujer, ¿bájase por aquí al Parral?"* My Spanish had never been so fluent; no, my face did not betray the slightest emotion. Yes, yonder was the rampart; behind it, the Eresma; that group of houses down there was El Parral. *"Bueno, gracias."*—*"¡Dios guarde a usted! ¡Y que no haya novedad!"* The good old woman!

The first thing I asked the keeper, when the gate of the convent opened on a fabulous garden, all abloom with almond-trees, so fresh, spring-like

Photo : L. Elton

SEGOVIA

(what a balm on my heart, and, at the same time, what a vain longing for that peace, so alien, so distant!)—the first thing, soon after having expressed my wish to see the church, was to ask the time. Had he said a quarter to eleven? *Bueno*, the alibi was at hand. Because at a quarter to eleven I was still in the cathedral, and the keeper's watch must have been at least a quarter of an hour late. "I thought it was earlier"—I was cheeky enough to add. "Nothing is left except the retablo and a few tombs": when in the church, I surprised myself reading for at least the third time this sentence in Baedeker. As for the retablo, you may guess what interest I took in it!

All I remember of El Parral is this: the blossoming cloister, the murmur of a tap, pools of water on the uneven floor (it had rained during the night, but the April morning had risen as glittering as a dewy flower), and graves, graves everywhere, some broken, some intact, and, everywhere, the tang of the fresh blossoms, as a season of paradise. I wanted the keeper to take me also to Vera Cruz. On coming back to the gate of the convent, a hurried knocking was heard from outside. "There!" I muttered to myself. The gate was opened. A peaceful, dark peasant carried in his arms a tender lamb, an armful of warm, soft wool. He exchanged a few words with the keeper. My eyes wandered from that soft armful of wool to the blossoming trees, so fresh, spring-like:

everything was light, everything was bright like those pools of water on the floor. A canary tried over and over again his festive trill, a spray of music which seemed to fill the air with a fountain of golden sparks. Water was trickling, gurgling, drop after drop, from the tap into the trough underneath. Was it possible? I wondered. Was it possible that such a thing should have taken place? And that *I* had done it? Was it possible? If they had asked me, that moment, I would have replied No, quite honestly. I was beginning to doubt myself the reality of what had taken place a few moments before in the cathedral.

How beautiful Segovia was, on that spring morning! Ramparts, houses, cupolas, towers, stood out so sharply, almost tangible in the crystal air, against the wide clean-washed sky, where the clouds tapered into golden banners! Snow-capped Sierra Guadarrama, on the left, enhanced the profile of the town, on that side; below, in the valley green with dark trees, here and there shot up the firework of some blossoming fruit-tree. The Alcazar, a turreted prow, no less improbable than the bewitched castles in Victor Hugo's drawings, seemed to propagate throughout the whole outline of the town a motion as of a living, blithe spirit. The town spoke in the sound of her bells. But with the sound of the bells—it was a merry sound, but its tempestuous rhythm

was enough to break the spell of the peaceful land‑
scape—the unwelcome thought again crept in. To
me that sound bespoke hurried steps, gathering
crowds, persecution, flight.

"In the case of riot or other popular disturbance,
the stranger should get out of the way as quickly as
possible, as the careful policemen, in order to pre‑
vent the escape of the guilty, are apt to arrest anyone
they can lay their hands on." Such is Baedeker's
advice. Had I to flee away? To rush to the hotel,
pack up, take the first train bound anywhere, give
up sight‑seeing in Segovia. . . . What if the hotel were
guarded by police? Of course, who else but a
foreigner could have raised the curtain? And at
what hotels would a foreigner put up if not at the
Comercio y Europeo or at the Paris? I was already
picturing to myself those so radical policemen men‑
tioned by Baedeker in the act of making a haul of the
whole party of Mr. Thomas, and cross‑examining
one by one all its members: a hypothesis which, in
spite of my worry, succeeded in cheering me. Then
it dawned upon me that in the confusion of the
previous night I had omitted to register my identity
at the hotel; for the police of Segovia I simply did
not exist. This circumstance seemed to me no little
indication of a benignant star.

Meanwhile the view of Segovia hovered over the
tempête dans mon crâne just as one of those vistas of

135

Paradise, framed in curled clouds, overhang the darkness and flames where the souls of Purgatory grope with outstretched arms. Oh, how sadly had I bungled my nice Spanish trip!

Along the Cuesta de los Hoyos, from the roadside some one suddenly bore down upon me. I was staggered. "¡Una perrita! caballero, ¡una perrita!" By me stood the gipsy, issued from the caverns to beg. I left the road, climbed a grassy slope. Something released a distant recollection. I was outside Urbino; I had but to turn round, to see the loggia of the Ducal Palace, between the two slender towers like a sheet of old parchment stretched between two rollers. But, from among the pines, it was Segovia Cathedral which towered in spaces ultramarine. Was I really the author of what had happened inside there?

When I entered the town again, by San Millán (it was half-past twelve) I was much calmer. At Plaza del Azoquejo, though, I thought some soldiers observed me with particular interest (I hated the uniforms, on that day). Their eyes went from me to the aqueduct, and from the aqueduct back to me. I guessed their thought: "Here is a foreigner; evidently he is gaping at El Puente. ¡Qué impertinente curioso!"

I avoided the main street, I made for the Casa de Segovia along a steep road. I wanted to get back to

SEGOVIA

the hotel by side-streets. From the top, one had glimpses over the tawny rain-polished terraced heights behind San Lorenzo; the sky was ultramarine, still with a threat of black sailing clouds. Everything on earth was fresh, spring-like.

At San Juan I met the whole party of Mr. Thomas; they were admiring Zuloaga's pottery. I anxiously scrutinised their faces: though I could hardly believe it, they did not betray any disturbing knowledge of what had happened in the morning. Their sight (oh, the coward gregarious animal man is, when in danger!) proved unusually sweet to me. Mr. Thomas—I looked at him with a sympathetic eye, I am sure. I mingled my remarks, in English, with those of the old spinsters I had disliked so much the day before. "Isn't it pretty this little vase?"—"Oh, look at the wonderful china!" I pointed out that the picture of one of the pieces of crockery was copied from the Madonna del Granduca. "I suppose you have seen it in Florence?" The old English lady was in raptures: "O yes, I see; my dear Madonna del Granduke, please, how much this, ¿cuanto?" The saleswoman quoted an exorbitant price. But I felt so full of goodwill towards the saleswoman, and towards the old spinster, and towards the horrid glazed crockery scrawled with steel-blue and Prussian-blue blots, and even towards Mr. Thomas. To speak with them made me feel one of them, caused me to merge my own responsibility in the group responsibility: I had never put to a more thorough test Jules Romains's unanimism. So, unburdened of my own ego, I thought I would disappear from before the others as I disappeared from before my-self: how possibly could the police detect *me*?

Now through winding streets the tourists, by twos and threes, proceeded to the Alcazar, Mr. Thomas taking the lead. I went so far as to approach Mr. Thomas and to ask him, in a friendly way, how well he had slept at the Madrileña. "It was all right, quite clean, of course"—he replied, slightly taken aback and distant. He blushed. Could I not mind my own business? Still, round his eyes the purple of shame was more vivid; there were tell-tale red spots, round the eyes and on the jaw of Mr. Thomas; there the Gillette blade had slightly scratched a very suspicious boil. "*Como si hubiera tenido sarampión*" —I was reminded of the old Spanish text: as if he had measles. "Have you been to El Parral? Wonderful, El Parral!" No, he had not visited El Parral; he had been to the cathedral. On hearing the cathedral mentioned, my pulse quickened. Rubbish! It was a dream. Mr. Thomas did not seem to connect any-thing sensational with the mention of the cathedral. Now I felt very effusive. I badly wanted to talk with everybody, to be trusted by everyone.—From some Spaniards, on the esplanade of the Alcazar, I asked

the name of a village one saw, white in the sun, beyond Vera Cruz. There was nothing remarkable in
that village. *"¿Es usted francés?"*—*"No, italiano."*—
"Italia es un país muy bonito"—stated one of them,
beaming. I wanted to hug him like a brother. Mr.
Thomas gathered his flock, and gave the order to
march to the hotel for lunch. By Santo Andrea rain
poured down. I kindly volunteered to shelter the
old spinster, defenceless against the shower, with my
umbrella. "So kind of you!" She also, for the moment, was very fond of Italy. But when I passed by
the cathedral I felt mightily impelled to enter it, to
see the violated altar—I was Raskolnikov climbing
the stairs of the accursed house, while a broad ruddy
moon gapes through the window.

Not a trace of policemen round the hotel; nobody
who bore the slightest resemblance to a detective. I
ate with a hectic appetite. But when, luxuriating
with a delicious cigar like a self-satisfied Sherlock
Holmes, I boldly showed myself in the doorway of
the hotel, out of the neighbouring Hotel Paris I saw
two persons coming and the sight was, to me, an un-
mitigated eyesore. They were the two foreign ladies
who had seen me enter the cathedral. The brown
frock, the three-cornered hat trimmed with feathers,
of the one, the mauve frock, the cloche, the spectacles of the other: there was no mistaking them.
There they were. And just they, now, after a first

movement of surprise (why was I sticking to the threshold, as if nailed?), just they came up to me. With a blush, the one with the three-cornered hat addressed me: "You have given us such a fright!" But the intonation of her voice, the gesture of her raised hand as if to warn a naughty child, and a vainly repressed smile harboured no enmity. I pretended the greatest of surprises, but the amused expression of my face told its tale. Why pretend? They had seen everything. They had seen me wriggle away from the church, they had guessed at once that I was the guilty one, and had wondered why the priests had failed to notice my presence. "You know, it has been awful! Awful!" At first, by that sound of thunder, they had thought of a terrorist's outrage; such must have been the general impression. The archbishop, poor old man, had grown as pale as a sheet, and had fainted in the arms of the deacons. "Think of it: it was just time for the Elevation of the Host. You horrid man!" (No doubt these ladies were protestant, since they seemed to relish such a monstrous sacrilege.) "You horrid man!" And she shook her jewelled finger as if to give a smack to a naughty child. But the real message I read in her eyes was: "Thank you! Such a thrill!" There had been frantic excitement. The whole of the clergy had run to the altar, the acolytes had been disposed in a cordon; all the gates had been closed by order.

That moment, Miss A.R.S. confessed to me afterwards, they had both sighed with relief at the thought that the guilty one had contrived to escape. But they had soon become very uneasy about their own fate. Shut in a church at the mercy of a furious clergy and a fanatic crowd, what would become of them, the only foreign people present? "You are laughing now, you horrid man, but I wish you had been there in our place!" Why, there was the altar, littered with rubble, and beneath the rubble the crucifix, the candlesticks and the prayer tablets lay, smashed. The dusty green curtain was stretched over those ruins like a flag over a warrior's body. But what about the sculpture itself? Oh, the sculpture had suffered no harm. Oh, well, in that case— But where had the rubble come from? I was wondering. (Those Spanish churches are a mystery to me. Everything seems to hold by a miracle of balance: mere inertia, I suppose, as anywhere else in Spain. Enough if you push the ramshackle thing with your finger: down they come, altars, hearses, friezes, like as many packs of cards! So I was thinking.) Perhaps the support of the curtain was a portion of the inside wall, who knows?

The priests ran to and fro like mad ants round their trampled hill. What were they saying in their harsh ejaculations? What were they arguing with their outstretched arms? "Better be still and keep

quiet in our place!'' So the two ladies had held their
peace in their seats in front of the *reja*, waiting. Miss
A. R. S. had felt in her purse for her British passport,
and thought herself safe under the shelter of the
Union Jack. And yet, when some of the peasants
had indicated them to an inquiring priest, when the
excited priest (he rolled his eyes, he gnashed his
teeth, he looked quite a brute!) had approached
them, followed by others, then assurance had failed
Miss A. R. S. She, also, had remembered Baedeker's
warning in the case of a riot or other popular disturbance, and had felt rather creepy. "*¿Francesa?*"
—the priest had sputtered, looking daggers. (In the
eyes of the staunch Spaniards whatever is sacrilegi-
ous is French, since time immemorial : "*¡Mueran los
Gabachos!*" Death for the miscreant dogs—was the
war-cry against Murat's French troops.) While her
companion, a Dutch lady, was trembling like an
aspen-leaf, Miss A. R. S. had replied in English,
with the calm of great occasions, that she wished to
see the cloisters. "*¿Francesa?*"—"Would you
kindly show us the cloisters?" A conversation could
hardly proceed successfully on these lines. The
priest, glowering at her with the terrible eyes of
Herrera's San Basilio, had pointed out the altar,
then he had directed his finger against the two
foreign ladies, grunting out incomprehensible
words. Miss A. R. S. avowed that, if she had been

able to talk Spanish, honestly she would have given me away; but how could she convey to the brute that the author of the sacrilege was "a gentleman who has gone through that door there, just a few moments ago, a gentleman with a hazel overcoat, a grey suit, and a grey felt hat with a dark ribbon, a young gentleman, clean-shaven, rather short. . . ." To start with, what was Spanish for gentleman? All she could do was to say: "*Caballero, sortido*," and to point to the door which I call the Gate of Salvation. The priest, however, must soon have been convinced that the outrage had not come from them. No doubt someone had seen them sitting the whole time in front of the high altar, and that one, now, spoke: it was a choir boy who had never taken his eyes off them, so much had he been engrossed in the presence of two funny foreign women rather than in the divine presence in the Host. However the incensed priest, before letting them go, had taken their names and address, so that they were still frightened, and imagined that the policemen would break in, any moment. If the policemen had actually come, and the ladies had denounced me, I was done. Done—perhaps I am exaggerating. After all, it was a matter of a few shards, which, even to pay them dear—yes, but did I know what Spanish priests might claim for a crucifix and a few paltry candlesticks, and a broken wall? Perhaps all the money I had for my Spanish trip would hardly be deemed sufficient. Besides, did not the ladies tell me that, on leaving the church, they had had the impression that the folk were terrified, and the priests themselves, unable to find a culprit, looked flustered and dismayed? "I am sure that they think it was due to some superhuman agency: they looked it. Oh, I know, they are an ignorant, superstitious lot! They think it is a miracle."

No wonder the two ladies were anxious to leave: they would go by the half-past five train to Madrid. So also was I. We would meet again in the train—or in the prison, if the police arrested us. I laughed aloud. Though I still had reason to fear, that conversation had braced me up. The sacrilege had dropped from me; I was myself again. Now the arrival of policemen would have struck me as unreal. The morning belonged to the past, had gone by. We parted rather cheerfully, like old friends. Our lively talk, which had taken place in the hearing of everybody (as if the Spaniards had been animals and not men) had awakened the curiosity of the old *dueño* of the hotel. After a few words on the weather (the sky had clouded again, and it was going to pour), he asked me what had I been laughing at, with the English ladies. I produced something plausible. He did not catch my words. He put his hand to his ear. I repeated. He shook his head. "*Yo también entendia algo el inglés—*" (So he

understood English, bless him!) *"Pero no oigo bien.
Tengo ochenta años, caballero. Oigo muy mal."*
Thank God, he was deaf!

Cheerfully under the first drops of the shower I
walked to El Puente (how beautiful it was now, El
Puente!), I skirted it until the arches disappeared
underground, I turned towards San Antonio El
Real (how graceful was that light frieze over the
gate!), in spite of the shower I went downhill, to
Santa Eulalia. I took shelter in a green-daubed gate-
way (that green daub looked so pleasant, so picturesque!). Guess at my relief when I said good-bye to
the Hotel Comercio y Europeo, think if I was
gallant when I said *au revoir* to the señorita (since,
no doubt, I would come back to Segovia; *¡me gustaba mucho!*), imagine my joy when I drove back to
the station (but, this time, not in the accursed *coche*,
but in one of the high-class buses labelled: MR.
THOMAS'S PARTY), picture my exultation when I
crossed the threshold of the station again (not a single
policeman, there!), got my ticket and took my seat
in the train! Miss A. R. S. was there, with her friend.
They said they still feared some unpleasant surprise
at the last moment, but I am sure that they said so in
order to prolong the thrill. In the Sunday afternoon
the Segovian policemen, to be sure, were all lying on
their backs, and would not have budged even if on
the surrounding hills all the tribes of Abd-el-Krim

had appeared in battle array. The Spanish altars are sacred, but Spanish idleness is more sacred still.

¡Viva la guardia civil,
Porque es la gloria de España!

"Anyhow, they might worry us in Madrid!"— said Miss A. R. S. when the train had started. I shook my head sceptically. The last thrill, the last feeble vibration of a spent earthquake, was provided by the sudden appearance of a policeman in our compartment; but the policeman was not after any-body in particular, and went by.

Miss Ann (let me at least mention her Christian name!) felt her soul refreshed, as a flower, warmed with the new sun, raises its trembling crown, and now gave vent to her Segovian impressions. Oh, what a delightful *parador* she had seen, with such a snow-white courtyard, and so many little rooms round the loggia, and, below, the mules in a row, tied to the columns, and such dark men, very pic-turesque, "sorry you missed it." She had longed so much for something really Spanish, and Burgos had been so depressing, swarming as it was with uncouth dwarfish soldiers at nightfall, and Valladolid had been just the same: soldiers, soldiers all the way; disgusting, really sickening. But at Segovia she had found the picturesque *parador*. And a picturesque thrill, too—I reminded her. "You horrid man!"

Now her smile was manifestly full of kindliness—of gratitude, I should say.

Dear Miss A. R. S.! In the Velázquez room, in the Prado, I was looking at the equestrian portrait of Prince Baltásar Carlos, when I heard behind me a voice I knew, exclaim: "Oh, look at the horse, he looks so stuffy, like a pin-cushion!" It was Miss Ann who was talking to her Dutch friend (Miss Ann called her Lily, and I, too, am going to call her Vrouw Lily, since I cannot remember her name bristling with repeated vowels like a misprint). After that, we frequently met, for the rest of the time we spent in Spain. We often came across each other in the Prado. Miss Ann made fun of El Greco, and turned up her nose at Rubens's nudes. One morning, in front of a certain landscape with fauns and nymphs, by the redundant Flemish master, we found a middle-aged French gentleman (obviously from the South) who, pointing out a naked steatopy-gous nymph in the act of crouching down with an arch look, cried out: "*Ah, c'est bien ça, Rubens! Moi j'aime cette femme-là!*" How she laughed, Miss Ann! Still, with a blush.

Because Miss Ann had lived long enough to remain under the last spell of Victorian prudishness, on the one hand, and, on the other, to look with an indulgent eye at the creeping license of American importation. Miss Ann had matured in a changing climate, and possessed also a changing charm, very personal. She dressed still with a slightly old-fash-ioned decorum. A poor Sevillian cicerone could not conceal his admiration for her regal manners (and one saw that the compliment was heartfelt); and the obese Jewess who had an antique shop in Gran Capitán, opposite Puerta de San Miguel, made no end of exclamations, when she tried the most valuable of her shawls (the eighteenth century *mantón de Manila*, black, with lively embroideries of Chinese style) on the shoulders of the magnificent Lady (who, like a stubborn child, ingeminated: "Don't touch me!"—so frightened was she by the fat grubby hands which arranged the shawl in folds; *"potius mori quam foedari"* is the motto you have with the ermine, Miss Ann!). Miss Ann's manners were really those of a great lady. If I possessed the naivety of a primitive painter, I would picture Iphigenia in Tauris exactly like Miss Ann, with the three-corn-ered hat trimmed with feathers, the pearl necklace round her rather long neck, the brown frock as solemn and graceful as a peplum, and her white gemmed hands waving in gestures both stately and sweet. After which of your eighteenth-century an-cestresses do you take, Miss Ann? In which family portrait gallery of a Queen Ann country house, drowsy in the midst of a wide green park, is that portrait hanging?

Yes, she was late Victorian; she loved South Kensington and would live part of the year in a quiet residential hotel of that slightly decayed neighbourhood, suggestive of an abandoned capital with its wide solitary streets. Because Miss Ann had no family of her own—only distant relatives, friends, acquaintances. She lived alone, but alone as only English people know how to live. During the winter on the Riviera, and in Switzerland for the sports (like most English people she was a devotee of Pontresina and Cadenabbia), for Easter, perhaps, in a villa overlooking Florence or the coast of Capri, in May, for the season, in London; during the summer sometimes in Norway or in Stockholm, sometimes in Salzburg for the Mozart festival. Autumn saw her in some English country house, staying with friends, and, again, in London. Such was the year of Miss A. R. S. Like most English people she had relatives scattered all over the world. She had American nieces, uncles living in India and in South Africa, cousins in Australia. She crossed Paris several times in a year: there she sometimes met with her overseas relatives. The American nieces would tease their spinster aunt about her Victorian reserve, and try to fluster her with cocktails (while a glass of vermouth was enough to make her feel dizzy); they would tell her the least probable of their adventures. Those confidences of lives so different from her own had bred in her a cardinal's soul, outside the world and at the same time acquainted with its ways, and accustomed to forgive much.

Miss Ann was living outside the world, somehow. She had renounced without taking vows. On an April evening we were sitting, I, Miss Ann, and Vrouw Lily, in one of those blossoming and enam‹elled corners of the Murillo Gardens at Seville. We had loitered along the immaculate lanes of the Barrio de la Cruz, we had lounged in the *patio* of the Irving Club and in those rooms slightly redolent of an old curiosity shop which the Marques de la Vega Inclán has newly redecorated for the greater glory of Spanish art. It was almost dark where we sat, but the lingering light had gathered in the evening sky arched above, soft and distant, shuddering at the budding stars. Was it Vrouw Lily who introduced the subject by urging Miss Ann to put on more clothes against the evening breeze? Or was it be‹cause those houses, behind the trees, shimmered white like cottages in the Riviera, and a little, also, like the walls of a hospital? Miss Ann had known the white cottages of the Riviera which every spring expose on their windows for a sun‹bath the mat‹tresses where somebody has died, in February, after having coughed for months and months (not too loud, though, in order not to shock the other guests); she had known the sudden wrapping up in the fur or

SEVILLE

The Giralda seen from the Patio de las Banderas

in the shawl, at the first shudder of the evening fever, and the hurried return home, while the sea-promenade is suddenly outlined by the row of lamps and the casinos kindle with the night fever, among the fiddling and clanging of the bands. Cannes, Mentone, Meran—Davos, too, she had known. A dear friend had died there; she had looked after that friend for a long time. Then it had come upon her, too, as if the dead friend had wanted her, clung to her still, as in the last days. Strain while managing a war hospital, a sudden breakdown, pleurisy. Now she also was recommended the blue train, rest, a sunny cottage by the Mediterranean, the whited sepulchre. Open air, substantial food, courage. At first she had been unable to rise from her bed. She was letting herself faint away, die. She *must* take interest in something. So she would cut the war bulletins and paste them in albums, ship-shape. She tried to forget her little tragedy in the big tragedy. But, indeed, only the fits of coughing were real; the bombardments were written on paper, and what did she care, after all, what did she care? Until one day courage had quickened within her, and she had really striven to walk, to breathe freely, to take food. The doctor wanted to send her to Davos. She had resisted the advice. She knew what Davos meant; she loathed the very name. She preferred to forget all that episode. Too much pity: it would have de-

stroyed what little grit she had left. Courage had
grown again within her, as if from a secret spring.
Little by little, by hardening herself, by disputing
the disease every inch, she had put on weight. With
suspended breath she would approach the weighing
machine, her oracle, week in week out. And now—
here she was, Miss Ann—as you see. And she smiled
in the dark; I felt she blushed with pleasure. She
had been born a second time. She had no family,
no children; she had been compelled to bring
herself into existence a second time, by herself; she
was the daughter of her own self. She had achieved
that: what more did they expect from their spinster
aunt?

She lived a little everywhere, she led a social life,
she let herself be booked up, as a matter of course,
for weeks ahead. Did she like that sort of life?
There are many ways of camouflaging the void, and
perhaps one is worth the other. And who profits by
seeing through it?

For the time being, Miss Ann had let herself be
convinced that Spain was the most picturesque
among the European countries. She also wanted
badly to see a really wicked Carmen. We sought her
in vain at the Fábrica Tabacos, the charming gipsy
girl, with the fiery carnation between her teeth.
*"Cinq mille Sévillanes! Des créatures si joliment faites
pour collaborer à des sensibilités raffinées, ne satisfairont*

que des simples sensualités." Autres temps, autres mœurs, o deliquescent Maurice. To-day the Fábrica Tabacos threatens to turn into an old-age hospice, and out of five thousand women you would not even find those fifteen beauties Pierre Louÿs was lucky enough to pick there. It seems that the State does not employ fresh people, and only allows those who have acquired rights to grow old there. There may have been a time when, perhaps, your refined sensibility would have been tickled by those now dishevelled worn-out females who, however, do not renounce the flower in their hair, were it only a withered one. *Cette odeur de décomposition* of which you are so *passionné*—this you would have found there, o deliquescent Maurice! But we were not refined enough to appreciate it; so we left with little regret those rooms alleged to be full of so many romantic stories of love, jealousy, desertion—as the tearful De Amicis has it—and misery: this last alone being still there. We sought Carmen in the Triana potteries; my scepticism secretly hoped to be given the lie. Triana: one of the capitals of the Peninsular Gipsyhood—there, if at all, Carmen ought to be found.

The Guadalquivir had put on its most tender robe tinted with the colour of rose-wood—*bois de rose*, last year's fashion, remarked Miss Ann ecstatically; and the half-naked scallywag who acted as a driver in the rickety taxi which we got, once across the bridge, showed very promising marks of thorough-bred gipsyness. But in the three or four potteries we visited we found only a subtle, sticky dust in the air, many-coloured porridges in the basins on the floor, like soups made with pease-flour, showrooms packed with industrial pottery not in the best of taste, with no trace left of the time-honoured craft, and, sitting at the long besmeared tables, plain girls, far less at-tractive than those who work in the Manchester cotton-mills. And yet we *must* find the wicked Car-men, or, at least, pretend to. Miss Ann, who hated disappointments, persuaded herself she had found her at last in an artist of a variety theatre in Sierpes. I did nothing to undeceive Miss Ann. I let her credit Dora la Cordobesita with the feelings rehearsed in these luscious lines:

> But in her room of curtains and plush chairs,
> She sits remembering her Matador—
> And roses crushed to red blood on the stairs . . .

You happy Miss Ann, who are still able to cherish your dear illusions, after all!

I still see you leaning out of the window of that little white house in Plaza del Museo where the Hotel de Inglaterra, being full, had found such charming rooms for you and your friend. True, the bed was a trifle uncomfortable and, during the night, at times, one felt somewhat funny (Vrouw Lily confided to me *sub rosa* that in her own bed she had found—exactly! "But do not tell Miss Ann: it would upset her!")—but the little square was so delightful and the landlady's daughter looked so much like one of Murillo's madonnas, so Spanish (though her father, as we happened to know afterwards, was a Swiss, Schneider by name). I still see you leaning out of that window, in the April morning, and I ask you from below: "Are you ready? It is just ten." And you put on your three-cornered hat trimmed with feathers, with such a sweet gesture, and smile to me (how young you do look, from here below!), and sing out: "Just a moment!" I am not quite sure whether on your window-sill there was a pot of red carnations, Miss Ann. Am I wrong? I knew there were none, still I see them:

> Arden claveles en tu cerco claro,
> Ardiente sangre, espléndidas heridas.

But that little pink house and the pea-green one, at the corner of that lane, those two houses so fairy-like, so crisp in the moonlight, they were there, you cannot deny it, Miss Ann; we have passed them many times, you, I, and Vrouw Lily, when I saw you home late at night, after having seen the real Carmen, the really wicked one, in that variety theatre of Sierpes,

frequented chiefly by foreigners—our authentic
Spanish night, culminating in a visit to that very
Spanish Pasaje de Oriente, all built in Moorish style.
No, though I have said it elsewhere, I cannot repeat
before you of what the Moorish style of the Pasaje de
Oriente reminds me; the Victorian soul within you
would blush, Miss Ann, and when you blush your
cheeks have two red spots like two roses which are
too red. Neither did I say what the magenta clusters
of the bougainvillæas recalled to me, that evening
we went to the Casa Pilatos. The tender crimson
sky and, in the shadow, the richly carved and stuc-
coed staircase, these are things whose recollection is
sweet. But as for the bougainvillæas which grow in
so many gardens along a beautiful and lugubrious
coast, it is better not to look at them. Do you smile?
I know that you are full of courage, and that it is I
who am being ridiculously sentimental, now; I know
that to your regal manners, answers a regal, energetic soul, trained in the school of a great Empire. I
know that you are not afraid of painful recollec-
tions. Forgive me, then, for these few pages. Do not
look at them as at something disrespectful—it is only
the whim of a sentimental youth, rather amusing (or
rather cruel?)—and forgive me, chiefly, for having
been unable to change the initials of your name, in a
work of fiction. Because those initials are yourself,
and wherever you may be now, at Wiesbaden, or at

Cairo, or at the Hague, or in some English country house drowsy in the midst of a wide green park, to write those initials I feel as if I were talking to you face to face—a thing which, for aught I know, may never happen again.

THE TRIUMPH OF DEATH

Putredini dixi: Pater meus es; mater mea,
et soror mea, vermibus—*Job*, xvii. 14

THE burly Archbishop in his purple vestments is
seated on the tall scarlet chair surmounted by two
plump baroque cornucopias. His face is as rubicund
as terracotta, his nose blooms like a cluster of purple
hyacinth.

The afternoon light, filtering through the slatted
shutters, fills the room with a ruddy opalescence as
of turbid amontillado, dimmed every now and then,
up there against the ceiling, by veils of sluggishly
moving dregs—the shadows of the passers-by, down
in the street. In the thick fleshy face of the Archbishop the eyelids, lowered on the watery eyes during the siesta, hardly stir, but from between his
teeth, at times, protrudes the tongue which ginger,
saffron, and cayenne have swollen like a parrot's.

Decidedly that Valencian chicken had been too
rich, and that *lomo de cerdo* too generous: the
draughts of *rioja* had been powerless to rout them.
Up they swam, again and again, those two inexorable
wrecks, with a garlicky sting in their wake.

Alas, Saint Joseph! Still, twoscore years' experi-

158

ence ought to have taught him the advantages of temperance, particularly on this day. José was his Christian name, so that the day of San José was the festival of both the meek old man holding a staff crowned with a lily, and of himself, the purple Archbishop whose crosier curled into a scaly dragon. Nestled in the crook of the crosier, Saint George pierced the throat of that dragon with his silver spear, just as he, the Archbishop, wished now to pierce the throat of the snake which, every now and then, would expand its coil within his chest till it nearly burst, and suddenly slacken and shrink with a whiff of poisonous fire. Ugh! His inside sickened at the thought of his crosier. While he pictured those scales, that dragon's crest, it was as if it gave a tangible form to his own distemper: all that yellow gold gave him a positive nausea.

Anyhow, the ceremony had been magnificent. Perhaps even more so than on any of the preceding years. The elaborate dressings and undressings had delighted him more than usual, and when the *Gloria in Excelsis* had flooded the deep aisles, he had indulged a sense of solemn elation. His gaze had wandered slowly over the whole vastness of the Cathedral. What brilliance! The Flemish reredos, all aglow behind four rows of candles, must have appeared like Paradise itself to the country-people who stared and gaped there, in the dusk be-

yond the glass screen of the *trascoro* which spared
the canons so many colds. And the concealed
electric lights, what an invention! His own inven‑
tion, of course. No other cathedral in Spain could
boast such illumination. Not even Toledo. Not
even Seville. But the mere thought of all that yellow
gold of lights, now, gave him a positive nausea. As
did also the neck of that snake which, once again, was
swelling to the bursting‑point in his chest. Ugh! A
devil of a snake, with its acid whiff— Then the whole
Chapter of Santa Maria la Real had come to offer
him its good wishes and compliments. There had
been a wonderful procession—the canopy over his
head stiff with gold embroidery (alas, too heavy, that
yellow gold!), and round him all that bluish smoke
of incense streaming upwards, and the chorus of
boys, while the sound of the organ burst out over
their heads like a thunderstorm.

Fray Jacinto, too, had preached splendidly,
though he had made a too lavish use of *hermanos de
mi alma, hermanos de mi corazón,* when he touched
the bottom of inspiration, and often had plunged
headlong into labyrinths of words without issue,
with *joyas místicas, sabiduría de contemplación, gozo,
suavidad y deleite, grandísima hermosura,* expressions,
evidently, all calculated to please him on his tutelary
Saint's day, since Fray Jacinto would not take his
basilisk eyes off him—eyes of a liverish missionary,

with a yellow cornea, so yellow indeed, that, to look at them, one felt positively sick. And the owl-faced beadle, with a rococo wiglet and that big belly which made him appear more broad than tall, was perched on the pulpit stairs, the mace in his hand, just like one of the monsters grinning in the capitals of the cloister, with big leafy bellies stuffed like those of Valencian chickens, pah!

Fray Jacinto's had been a splendid sermon, but he, José Carranza, used to preach better. Not without reason was he called *príncipe de nuestros oradores, el orador por antonomasia*, the descendant of the great seventeenth-century preachers, he who had inherited Cornelio's wisdom, Baeza's depth, Duleta's wit, Silveyra's learning. His delivery had been praised as *crespa, sonora, retumbante*; it made some think of the sermons of Santo Tomás de Villanueva for the natural tone, the combination of suavity and forcefulness, others, of those of Padre Antonio de Vieyra for the novelty of the subjects, the felicity of the evidence, the delicacy of thought, while most, after having heard him, no longer regretted having been born too late to hear Fray Luís de Granada, that Spanish Demosthenes. He preached with such power and zeal, that he filled even the most obdurate hearts with terror. During a famous sermon he had preached in Oviedo, not a single cough or sneeze had broken the silence of the immense congregation, such was the engrossment of the multitude in his words. Another time, on an Ash Wednes-day, at Palencia, he had preached on the dis-solution of the body with such eloquence, that the whole congregation had begun to shiver with a sort of tremor similar to the shudder of a raging calenture—

"*Memento, homo, quia pulvis es, et in pulverem re-verteris.* Consider, my dear brethren, how God has made us of mud, ashes, and a still filthier matter, the lewd slime of lust of the lower belly. Man pursues the works of the flesh, and has no flesh, since his flesh is but dust held together with plasters; man loves robes more fragrant than precious spikenard, while his only natural garment is the winding-sheet that grows with him from his conception, grows every hour until it consigns into the hands of Death the lump of dank mud inside, which has been wasting away every hour. *Nullo non se die extulit.* It dies every day, it lives never unto life, but lives and dies unto death. We all consume away and die; and, what is worst of all, we blindly rush headlong into Eternity, whence there is no return. 'And all the days that Adam lived were nine hundred and thirty years: and he died.' 'And all the days of Seth were nine hundred and twelve years: and he died.' 'And all the days of Enos were nine hundred and five years: and he died.' 'And all the days of

Methuselah were nine hundred sixty and nine years: and he died.' Consider, my dear brethren, what we were in our mother's womb: a filthiness fed with such impure blood as would parch the soil, blight the plants, and madden the dog which should drink of it. Consider what each one of us is now: a volume of diseases bound up together, a senescent child, a hoary baby, still longing to prolong his progressive corruption, until the heart grows faint, the head shaky, the spirit languid, the breath ill-smelling, the face wrinkled all over, the eyes dim, the nostrils dripping, the teeth rotten, the ears deaf, the hair scanty and white. And still some of us besmear their decayed beauty with a lying *fucus*, fill their cheeks with ceruse, and let their head lack no ointment, as if to deceive themselves as to what is beneath the wrinkled skin, what in the corrupted liver, and in the sinks of the body. They are like dunghills covered with snow, and all the perfumes and ointments they spend upon their diseased body are like menstruous rags upon a skin of leprosy. If man were fully aware of the corruption and rottenness, which are his sole and universal patrimony, he would never set his heart on the joys of the flesh, which are won with toil, held with anxiety, and lost with grief, but he would rather fix all his pleasure, love, care, desire and thought upon God, so that Death might not find him keeping company with

Sin, which is filthy, rough as a porcupine, black as the shadow of the night.

"Consider, my dear brethren, the grass and the trees of the fields. They bring forth flowers, leaves, and fruits, but man brings forth lice, caterpillars, and vermin, and such filthiness that 'He who is of pure eyes cannot behold.' *Cuius vulturis hoc erit cadaver?* What vulture, what cancer, what wolf shall feed on this rotten body, on this festering sore? *Cum autem morietur homo, haereditabit bestias, serpentes et vermes.* Moths and worms shall have him. The moth shall eat him up like a garment, and the worm shall eat him like wool. We must all pass through this posthumous death, this death after death, this dissolution after dissolution, this death of vermiculation and incineration, when those bodies that have been the children of royal parents, and the parents of royal children, must say with Job, 'Corruption, thou art my father,' and to the worm, 'Thou art my mother and my sister.' Miserable riddle, when the same worm must be my mother and my sister and myself. Miserable incest, when I must be married to my mother and my sister, and be both father and mother to my own mother and sister. While alive, man breeds lice and vermin, when dead he brings forth worms and flies. And the worm shall feed, and feed sweetly upon man, and he shall be turned unto a stink, first, and then he shall not be able to send forth so much as an ill air, not any air at all, but shall be all insipid, tasteless, savourless dust. One dies in the prime of life, being full of company and servants, and wholly at ease, and another dies in the bitterness of his soul, this man dies laughing, and the other dies weeping, but they both shall die infallibly, both shall lie down alike in the dust, and the worm shall cover them and be spread under them. These are the dais and the carpet that lie underneath, these the baldaquin and the awning that overhang, the greatest of the son of men, until at the Day of Judgment they all shall be summoned from their charnel-houses to the presence of the terrible Judge, and all that troubled their conscience, and all that they willingly forgot, shall be proclaimed by the trumpet of God, by the voice of an Archangel, in the great congregation of Spirits and Saints."

Here comes the Ash Wednesday procession. Look at the capirotes and the long hoods of the Nazarenes! They carry Death's emblems, the cross-bones, the skulls crowned with tiara, diadem, mitre, all the crowns of the princes of the world and of the princes of the Church. None of the Nazarenes utters a word. Each one of them keeps a rigid finger stretched against the motto of the label which accompanies each skull: *Finis Gloriæ Mundi, Via Omnis Carnis, Ludibria Mortis, Nemini Parco, OmniaÆquat*—None of them speaks, but now one,

now another, strikes the ground with his tall iron
staff, and that sound freezes one's bones like the icy
chill of death. The pageant seems longer than usual,
this time; and why the officers in full uniform, with
parti-coloured trousers and the long mantles of the
orders of knighthood, why that coffin carried on the
shoulders of the dignitaries? And, in the open coffin
which comes nearer and nearer, who is that priest in
his purple vestments, with a swollen face disfigured
by subcutaneous injections, so that it might not sag
like an obscene jellyfish, who is he but the Archbishop José Carranza, the same who, lost among the
crowd, watches the scene with a lump in his throat?
A lump, the coil of a yellow snake, a worm expand-
ing its segments until his breast should burst—a
bolus clogs his throat, a bolus of bitter garlicky
medicine they have put there, in order that the
bottle of rotten humours into which his body is
turned may not leak and overflow—

ÆTERNITAS

Nuevo Procedimiento para la Conservación y Embalsama-
miento de Cadáveres

SIN INTERVENCIÓN QUIRÚRGICA ALGUNA.

SIN QUITAR LA ROPA DEL CADÁVER.

RESPETANDO SU SAGRADA INTANGIBILITAD.

TARIFAS

Equipo corriente letra A .	.	.	Pesetas 1500
Equipo de 1ª letra B .	.	.	Pesetas 2000
Equipo especial letra C .	.	.	Pesetas 3000

VALDÉS LEAL   *Photo : Anderson*

Las Poſtrimerias de la Vida

Seville : Hospital de la Caridad

The humours are shaken like bilge-water, in the sinks of his body, at every jerk of the coffin: if only the bearers would stop walking with that rocking military gait! Accursed Spanish streets, only fit for mules, not for an Archbishop's carriage! *"Cuidado, Juan. ¡No me gusta volcar!"* But Juan the coach-man is not here; there is no carriage, but a coffin. The dead Archbishop is livid; his appear-ance is sickening. José hides his face on the shoulder of his mother, who has taken him in her arms to watch the spectacle. José is a good *niño*, and mummy has taken him to the Archbishop's funeral, because José is very fond of religious ceremonies. José is going to be a priest, but now he suffers from worms and dizziness. José must keep very quiet; mummy touches his forehead; José has got a little tempera-ture, to-morrow he will be given a purge. Ugh! the worms crawl up to his very throat! Then he will go to bed. How restful it is to be in bed, chiefly when the bed is so tall, with so many candles all round! Too many candles around, too much gold, too much yellow. But it is no bed at all, it is a catafalque, and José is the Archbishop lying in state on the cata-falque, in the midst of a chanting and crooning mul-titude. When the show is over, they will lay him down in the sumptuous granite and bronze tomb, and there, at last, the humours will cease to seethe, be-cause granite is firm, it does not jerk like a coffin;

and all round there will be no longer that infinite flicker of yellow lights which shoot to and fro ceaselessly, like a dance of corposants. So many candles, too many candles! At least, electric light does not glimmer like that. This is why he devised the concealed electric lights: *"una iluminación muy mística, la mas sugestiva de España"*—El Sol, 20 jenuario 1922 (*Nuestro Servicio particular*).

> Esta que admiras fábrica, esta prima
> Pompa de la escultura, oh caminante,
> En porfidos rebeldes al diamante,
> En metales mordidos de la lima— [1]

How beautiful it is, the Archbishop's tomb, in the corner of the chapel! From that corner he will overhear the services until doomsday. And the inscription, a very appropriate one:

> Y esa inscripción consulta que elegante
> Informa bronces, mármoles anima— [2]

---

[1] Edward Churton's free translation of this sonnet of Góngora's runs:

> Stranger, this beauteous fabric, last and best
> Of sculpture's triumphs, canopies, that shine
> With porphyry bright as diamonds from the mine,
> With metals rich inlaid . . .

[2] . . . Go, read the line
> Graven on that tomb, affection's generous sign,
> That on the breathing marble hath impress'd
> His reverend name . . .

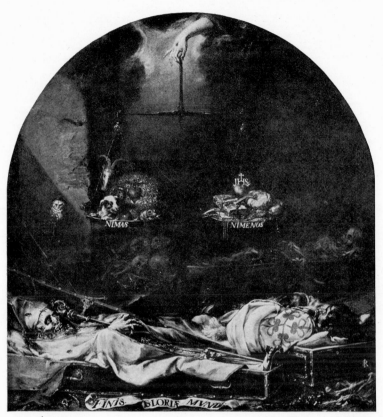

VALDÉS LEAL Photo : Anderson

Finis Gloriæ Mundi

Seville : Hospital de la Caridad

And the crest all alive with colours, *or five mullets azure*:

> ... a un campo de oro cinco estrellas
> Dejando azules con mejores plantas
> En campo azul estrellas pisa de oro.[1]

Too vivid, that yellow gold. Tone it down! Tone it down! Ugh! Ugh! It is stifling inside the tomb; the body has swollen to the point of touching the walls from all sides: will the stone burst asunder?

JOSEPHO.CARRANZAE

NAVARRO.DOMINICANO

PRÆSULI SANCTISSIMO

VIRO GENERE.VITA DOCTRINA.CONCIONE

ATQ.ELEEMOSYNIS CLARO

ANIMO IN PROSPERIS MODESTO

IN ADVERSIS ÆQUO

OBIIT ANNO. . . .

ÆTATIS SUÆ. . . .

AD SONUM.TUBÆ.ARCHANGELI

EXPECTAT.INDUERE

IMMORTALE

The stone has cracked; the crevice runs throughout the whole length of the inscription. One feels

[1] He leaves this earthly blazon of his race,
   Five azure stars in golden field, to tread
   In field of liquid azure stars of gold.

sucked in, dizzily. Shooting downwards, spinning,
reeling. The worms. Children, do not eat too much,
says the doctor. A thousand miles a minute, head⸗
long through the crust of the earth, till at last, at the
bottom of the pit, a yellow light, dim, distant at first,
nearing speedily.

Upside⸗down, the Archbishop José hangs over an
inferior world, lit by a saffron light issuing from a
big cauldron as huge as a gasometer. The fire reeks
of garlic. And the vast panorama teems with a
loathsome life, white things like lice. They are
skeletons. Skeletons everywhere. How horrible,
skeletons moving about like living men! Armies of
skeletons. A phalanx of them, there: the picked
skulls glint like helmets. Those of the first rank hide
behind tall rectangular shields: coffin⸗lids. Six
shields abreast, six coffin⸗lids: behind them, ranks
and ranks, ten thousand deep. Those of the first
rank peep from behind the shields, as if from behind
screens; they are smirking. The phalanx is marking
time. Presently they will march on, lock⸗step, foot
after foot, file after file, over those troops of men, a
drunken, wounded, swooning, chained, crowd
scattered there in front of them. Some of those men
dare to feast. A table is laid; and, on it, a Valencian
chicken, a loin of pork; away, away, with those
loathsome dishes! They guzzle and swill, hurriedly,
filthily. Their shrieks reach up here: angry vul⸗

PETER BRUEGHEL   *The Triumph of Death* (Detail)

Photo : Anderson

170]

tures fighting for a lump of raw meat. Or is it the sound of the guitar in the hands of that wretch whose head rests on the breast of a courtesan? Why does that one in black draw his sword? Against whom? Will he be mad enough to oppose Death armed with a scythe, who rides at full speed on a skeleton horse? They fall hither and thither in their flight, the miserable fugitives, with grotesque tumbles as in a sack-race. But Death drives them with his scythe towards a huge trap on whose roof another Death, a gigantic one, beats the kettledrums with such a noise that one feels deafened and dizzy. The roof of the trap is a coffin-lid; the trap is a big coffin, as big as a church. Two sinister skeleton sextons drag a mummy in a wheeled coffin, and run over a corpse swathed tight in a winding-sheet like a new-born child. A king draped in ermine has dropped his nerveless sceptre-holding arm, spell-bound by the sand-glass which a skeleton keeps before his eyes. Another Death carries in his arms a cardinal like a limp menstruous rag; another tramples a crumpled abbot. Ugly monsters move about here! Some have chicken legs, some seem to be made of vegetables: the backbones are cabbage stalks, the knuckles are as shiny as leeks, the skulls as glossy as bulbs of garlic. On a dung-cart, to the sound of a passing bell, a painstaking Death heaps bleached skulls; a stale stench exhales from them.

A martello tower spits out another band of skeletons draped in snow-white shrouds. They gather on a battlement and blow long trumpets; a green swollen corpse floats in the moat below; a Death grinning with a cruel rictus peeps at regular intervals, cuckoo-like, out of the clock of the tower above. Further, the valley bristles with scythes, spears, halberds: more battalions of skeletons for warfare and slaughter. On the top of a hill, the enceinte of a house is full of running skeletons, who scurry round and round until the door bursts open; from the slope below a funeral cortège climbs up, preceded by a cross. The tops of all the hills are covered with dead bodies, beheaded by gaunt executioners, hanging from tall gallows, stuck on raised grids, nailed to stricken trees, hurled down gaping precipices, roasted in brazen turrets. In the distance, the darkened sea is full of shipwrecks amidst volcanic archipelagoes, and the coast, dotted with dead trees to the livid sky-line, is all ablaze with black and sulphur flames.

But below, perpendicularly, is the huge cauldron, watched by a phalanx holding long, smoky torches; and the black sprawling shapes afloat on the liquid fire are men; how fearfully they thrust their faces upwards and roll their yellow eyes! *Pedro, ¡no me mires así! No me mires así, ¡Pedrillo! No tengo culpa.* Do not stare at me like that, it was not I. I

PETER BRUEGHEL   *The Triumph of Death* (Detail)

Photo : Anderson

172]

will take care of your widow, I will see to the educa_stion of your children. The *onzas* are still inside the crucifix; I swear to you, it was your father's authentic will. *Piedad de mí, ¡Pedrillo!* It was not I who caused him to disinherit you. Help! Alas, my foot holds no longer on that pendulous root. It is getting looser and looser. Presently I shall fall headlong into that yellow fire! Now the humours remain no longer bottled in my body. What is going to happen, O! *Jesumaria*, those are no eyeballs: what peeps out of each eyesocket is a worm, a glossy worm. Now he is gazing at me also from above. Ah, it is he who is sawing the root! Away, Pedrillo! *¡Piedad de mí!* The yellow fire singes my hair. . . . Even the pitch_sfork, you rascal! even the pitchfork you push against my throat, so that I may fall the sooner! Oh God, I am choking, help! . . .

The Archbishop stares at the room. Now the room is full of a sulphurous light, since one of the shutters has been thrown open by the wind, and the March sun, already hot, hits his forehead. He passes his hand over his forehead: it is wet with cold sweat. The clammy tongue in his palate is as bitter as a bolus of aloe. Alas, Saint Joseph! For the last twenty years, at least, the festival has been causing him such troubles. Temperance! Moderation! The Archbishop José Carranza is as yellow as bile; his purple nose is turned into a pale-blue cluster of hyacinth. He leans on the arms of his chair, stands up. As swiftly as the bulk of his body allows him, he crosses the room, and, pressing the handkerchief against his mouth, walks out through a small door.

MYSTICISM,
OR ADVOCATUS DIABOLI

MYSTICISM,
OR ADVOCATUS DIABOLI [1]

πολλοὶ μὲν ναρθηκοφόροι, παῦροι δέ τε Βάκχοι.
—*Orphic text*

Mr. Broadway—Just think of it: three hundred mystical writers and three thousand or more of their works! Isn't it wonderful? An actual ocean of mysticism, *oceanum mysticum*. An inexhaustible mine. To think that while the *conquistadores* went through the toil and moil of a perilous voyage to load their galleons with the ill-gotten spoils of the Indian kingdoms, an army of saints, at home, were storing for us a much less perishable treasure, the gold and gems of their mystical experiences—Great Spanish mystics, divine knight-errantry bent on the conquest of the Kingdom of Heaven, which delighted in suffering their violence!

Mr. Narrowgate—Certainly the blossoming of mysticism in Spain during the sixteenth and seventeenth centuries is no less of a wonderful phenomenon than the religious revival in Italy during the thirteenth century. Mysticism was, so to say, in

[1] Both the interlocutors of this dialogue appear here and there indebted to Jean Baruzi's excellent study on *Saint Jean de la Croix et le Problème de l'Expérience Mystique*, Paris, Alcan, 1924.

the air. But, my dear Broadway, you won't forget that, whenever a current happens to be so predominant as mysticism was in Spain during that Golden Age, a fair number of imitators and impostors is to be expected. You do not ignore, I suppose, that cases of people, chiefly women, boasting supernatural intercourse were of almost everyday occurrence during that period. Some may have been victims of self-deception, but I am sure that most of them simply faked a religious experience. Think of the many charlatans who flourished during the century of Lights! On the other hand, how many inferior spirits are likely to have aped the language of the few great ones! They would adopt a phraseology which implied much more than the actual experiences they had undergone. They did it in good faith, I grant you, but, all things considered, I am sure that the big number of three hundred mystics is greatly exaggerated, and that the figure which is given for their works is absolutely unreliable.

Mr. Broadway—Still, no less an authority than Menéndez y Pelayo has given it. However, even granting that the estimate is rather too high, there are enough mystics left to make of that age an age of wonder. And, after all, there is nothing incredible in that phenomenon. It is only too natural that it should have taken place in Castille. The very appearance of the desert-like plateaux was calculated to give to the minds of the inhabitants a mystical bias. I was reading just the other day what Count Keyserling has written on the cosmic, stellar element in the Castilian landscape: the expanse of star-spangled heavens ought to be much more of a living reality to the Castilian than the dreary featureless wilderness of the barren plateaux. Remember what a supreme rôle night plays in St. John of the Cross and Luís de León. When I think of the Castilian landscape, I understand Spanish mysticism, just as I understand the *Edda* and Ibsen's theatre when I think of the gloomy gorges of Måbödal or Nærödal. In Norway the soul feels almost sucked in by the gaping sunless gulfs, in Spain she is rapt to the sky. Besides, the admixture of Arab blood in the Spanish race favoured the rise of mysticism. Unfortunately I know too little of the Arab mystics, but I hear that they reached the sublimest heights, and that the religious poetry of the West is like a child's stammer when compared with the flights of Ibn 'Arabî.

Mr. Narrowgate—I do not call in question the movement as a whole. Only I wish to discriminate. I am afraid your statistics would come down to a much more reasonable figure on closer inspection. Let us say that there are perhaps about two score or so of Spanish religious writers who have a claim to be called mystics. All depends on what you mean by mysticism.

Mr. Broadway—I seem to have read a few years ago, in some book by an Anglo-Catholic, a definition of mysticism which struck me as satisfactory enough. That writer concluded by saying that a mystic is one who has fallen in love with God.

Mr. Narrowgate—I cannot agree with your Anglo-Catholic author. Why, can one call that a definition? Love of God is proper to every religious experience, from the lowest to the highest degree. Of course there are infinite shades of love, but, then, the problem is shifted to the meaning of love, and your definition has hardly advanced. There is devo-tion, there is asceticism, and there is meditation; but though you cannot deny that the devout soul, and the ascetic soul, and the soul addicted to such meditations as those advised by St. Ignatius, are in a measure filled with the love of God, you will grant that a meditation or a prayer, even a high form of prayer, are quite distinct from contemplation proper, and from that highest contemplation which is the supreme stage of the Mystic Way. Generally what goes under the name of mysticism is only a more complex form of prayer.

Mr. Broadway—I see that you put meditation rather on a low rung in your ladder. Do you imply that Saint Ignatius was no mystic?

Mr. Narrowgate—There is an irreconcilable contradiction between such meditations as those St.

Ignatius enforces in his *Spiritual Exercises* and the mystic's progress. St. Ignatius's technique is calcu‹ lated to develop the sensory imagination: you fix your attention on the thought of the flames of Hell, until you actually feel their scorching heat on the palms of your hands; you picture the place where Christ was scourged until you actually revive in yourself that moment of the Passion. This method, as you know, is called by St. Ignatius "composition of place." But this kind of experience is part and parcel of the world of the senses, that world which a true mystic like St. John of the Cross strives to ex‹ clude. St. Ignatius's is a plastic method, St. John of the Cross's is just the opposite. Ignatius's so‹called art of contemplation, in reality a sensuous prayer, concrete to the point of paroxysm, would be a strange way indeed to reach that "general and obscure contemplation," that *noticia amorosa general* indicated by the Carmelite saint! One may be sure that many of the trials St. Teresa had to endure were brought about by the wrong type of prayer, the Ignatian prayer, enforced upon her by her spirit‹ ual directors. To be quite frank, I think that the Ignatian method results naturally in those emblems and divine devices of which there was such a large output during the seventeenth century. St. Teresa, in an Ignatian mood, saw the devils playing with her soul as with a ball, *"jugando a la pelota con el alma"*:

your Jesuit emblem-writers actually represented similar scenes in neat engravings, for the benefit of the devout souls committed to their care. Take, for instance, the most popular of them, Hermannus Hugo, from whom Quarles derived his quaint emblems——

Mr. Broadway—All this is very well, but St. Ignatius beheld visions, was subject to ecstasies. There is positive historical evidence for it. What, for instance, about his eight days' trance at the Hospital of St. Lucy? You must grant that ecstasy is a sure enough test. In fact, there lies the very essence of mysticism.

Mr. Narrowgate—Yours is the current view about mysticism. There are many current views about mysticism. Most people do not know of what they are talking when they talk of the mystical experience. They feel rather attracted by the notion of ecstasy: a thrilling adventure, a tête-à-tête with God. I see your Marble Arch audience relishing the gross yarn spun out by some half-witted woman or some besotted old man. The woman who talked with Christ; rather fine, eh?

Ecstasy represents a very inferior plane of mystical experience. It is, in fact, the result of a clash between our normal nature and a mysterious exaltation of the soul. It is the spectacle of the repressed senses trying to find a vicarious outlet and working in the void.

They were on the look-out for a gratification, and they found an excuse for rushing to the wrong appeal; but they do not apprehend any substance. Hence the swoon, the ecstasy. Therefore St. John of the Cross is very severe in his indictment of ecstasies, dreams, visions: they all belong to the phenomenal world. Raptures, transports, bodily dislocations, they always intervene when the communications are not purely spiritual. This is what St. John of the Cross says in his *Night of the Spirit*. The mystic who indulges in them goes astray, leaves the main road to pure contemplation. No wonder ecstasy was popular during the seventeenth century, the century in which, more than in any other age, intellect, as an English critic has said, was on the tip of the senses. But while the "spirit of sense" may be fruitful in art, it bears very dubious fruits in religion. Not without reason, I think, was the Inquisition very severe with people who professed to be subject to ecstasies, to talk with God and the Saints.

Mr. Broadway—But all the great mystics had some trouble with the Inquisition. St. Teresa had; and St. John of the Cross, too. And Luís de León—

Mr. Narrowgate—If the Church canonised the two Carmelite saints, it means that there was more in them than ecstasies and raptures. After all, those supreme tensions of the body and the soul are prevented from lasting long by the very lack of equilibrium from which they spring. St. Teresa reckons half an hour the time during which she was in a trance; Pascal says that the soul is incapable of maintaining itself for long on that level; it can only reach it to fall back again. No, the ecstasies alone are insufficient to make a saint in the eyes of the Church; but I am satisfied with the thorough investigation of the lives and works of those great mystics the Church made before canonising them. On the other hand, I do not believe that, because St. Ignatius was canonised, he was necessarily a mystic. There is Leah, and there is Rachel. There are militant saints and contemplative saints, and I think that St. Ignatius belongs to the former class. I think, also, that the former class is by far the larger one; and that the contemplative life of the mystic is "such a heroic and rare deed," as it has been said, such a brave thing it is, that I, for myself, would be extremely strict in examining the claims of those forty or fifty religious authors who are supposed to form the pick of Spanish mysticism.

Mr. Broadway—I see, you start from perfection, or nearly so, and you look down, but I would rather start from the lowest forms and look up. Not all those who have gone through the trials of the "night of sense" succeed in entering the "night of the spirit," and fewer still are those who, after traversing the night of the spirit, reach the stage of divine

union. There are infinite degrees of incomplete-
ness, but, if a constant effort towards an ultimate end
counts for something, imperfect mystics deserve no
less the name for having been unable to attain beyond a comparatively low degree. Perhaps during
the whole of their lives they were struggling with an
internal whirlwind of aspiration, never able to soar
on its wing. Mystics in the making, saints *in fieri*,
thwarted in their heroic effort, living in a state of
unrequited desire, save, perhaps, for sporadic moments in which they felt near to the goal. Would
you deny the name of mystics to these dusty and
bleeding athletes of the Faith? And, after all, do you
really find actual perfection? Is not there always
some trace of a former stage, of a lower degree, even
in the most proficient of mystics? History supplies
you with a confusion of data, from which it is perhaps just possible to establish a theoretical idea, a
canon of what mysticism should be; but you will
hardly find that canon thoroughly embodied in any
of the historical mystics. Think of what happens in
another field, not very distant from mysticism. I
mean poetical inspiration. Would you admit to
Parnassus only the three or four very great poets,
and leave the others, the minor ones, in the outer
darkness? And, as for the great ones, you will
grant that even Homer is found nodding sometimes.

Mr. Narrowgate—I do not think that your paral‹
lel is very satisfactory, but let us consider it all the
same, for a moment. Well, verse is not necessarily
poetry; in the same way, writing on the love of God
is not necessarily mysticism. As for the admission to
Parnassus, may I set up another quotation from
Horace against yours? "Poets are not permitted to
be mediocre." Neither are mystics, in my opinion.
Aspirants are little good. Minor verse may be in‹
teresting in many other respects, say as a literary
document, or as evidence bearing upon certain
aspects of a fashion, but would you have recourse to
it for your daily comfort and inspiration? That is
the test. I would be very strict indeed in admitting
people to Parnassus. I feel like an old republican
Roman, in this matter; I do not like the Roman
franchise to be made cheap.

Mr. Broadway—The criterion of admission must,
in any case, be less strict for mystics than for poets.
It is not difficult to obtain evidence of earnestness
and sublimity in poetry; but it is, on the contrary,
extremely difficult to be thoroughly satisfied about
mysticism. You see, the poem is there, you can al‹
most walk round it, examine it in all its details; the
proof of the union with the Muse is as clear as day‹
light. But the union of love with God is an experi‹
ence which beggars description; you must take
much for granted, and be content with a presump‹

tion instead of a proof. The autobiography of a mystic is not necessarily a guarantee of the secret of his soul. This could happen only if mystics were capable of self-criticism. But critical speculation is incompatible with the spontaneous movements of religious thought and sentiment. Take even the greatest of Spanish mystics, St. John of the Cross. He is very precise in the elimination of whatsoever is illusion; but when he comes to the great experi-ence of the soul becoming divine, his language fails him. The transposition of the experience is only partially achieved. His account of the Mystic Way is incomplete. Both the *Ascent of Mount Carmel* and the *Dark Night* come abruptly to an end just on the threshold of the supreme stage. Was he afraid of reducing his supernatural experience to the level of a phenomenon of the sensible world? Be that as it may, nobody is likely to dispute that St. John of the Cross is a mystic, and a great one, at that. Why should we deny to the mystic writer what we accept as normal in a poet or a novelist? Do we not allow poets and novelists to screen from our eyes their empirical existences?

Mr. Narrowgate—Ah, but pardon me—there is a great difference. As you say, for a poet or a novelist we have evidence, a justification of their claims. The work of art is there, and, again, the work of art is all. The life is of little or no importance. But if the mystic says nothing of *his own* experience, what evidence have we that he is entitled to be called a mystic? The experiences of actual life, in an artist, are of value only in so far as they are transposed into a work of art; he is an artist only on account of his work. But a mystic is a mystic only on account of his life as seen through his writings or any other evidence available. And his work has an edifying value only if it is actually based on experience. We know that the work of St. John of the Cross is a confession of the unique history of his life, transposed into a symbol. The work, in the case of the mystic, is primarily a document. Whoever has a claim must support it somehow, what do you think?

Mr. Broadway—Well, if it is for confessions, you would probably get plenty of them in the case of the *alumbrados*. They never tire of describing the progress of their souls in glowing words. And still, they are pseudo-mystics, condemned by the Church. As you said a few moments ago, to write on the love of God does not necessarily mean to be a mystic.

Mr. Narrowgate—Yes, the *alumbrados* are beyond the pale. Still, distinction between them and the proper mystics is not so easy to draw as you would expect. You may think you have discovered a good criterion in the presence of quietism in the *alumbrados*, in their indulgence in the gratifications of the emotions. However, when St. John of the

Cross takes refuge in a general, obscure contempla‑
tion, he is on the outskirts of illuminism, nearly *sapit
heresim*. He steers free of it; true, he does not get
lost in the troubled regions of affective life. But illu‑
minism, there is no denying it, has played a far from
secondary part in the development of Spanish
mysticism. However the position of the *alumbrados*
need not detain us now. My point is only this. As
you realise yourself, it is extremely difficult to distin‑
guish a true from a pseudo‑mystic. I would not for a
moment think of including the *alumbrados* in the
roll of the mystics. Better to be too exclusive than
too inclusive. Our roll of mystics will be the shorter
in consequence of this strict principle, but all the
more sterling for that. One can be a holy man with‑
out being a mystic, and I hope we do no great in‑
justice to Fray Hernando de Talavera, to Alejo de
Venegas, and to Hernando de Zarate if we classify
them among the ascetic and theological writers
rather than among the mystics. They have flashes of
inspiration, but if we include them in our roll on
account of those flashes, we should have to grant
admission to such a legion of religious writers that
mysticism would lose its proper, specific meaning.
In short, I stick to the definition of mystic life given
by pseudo‑Dionysius: the three characters of passi‑
vity, obscurity, dispossession, ought to be recognis‑
able.

Mr. Broadway—If you are going to apply this rule to Spanish mysticism, I am afraid I cannot follow you. Since the Spanish mystics are different from the others; they played great rôles in active life, they were militant saints, with little of the metaphysician in them. So you see once again the necessity of keeping to the broad side in the definition of mysticism.

Mr. Narrowgate—Indeed the greatest of them, St. Teresa and St. John of the Cross, were active, militant saints. But do not confuse the character of their outer with that of their inner life. I do not think there is any contradiction between a militant life like that of St. Teresa or St. John and mysticism as defined by pseudo-Dionysius.

Mr. Broadway—But what were you saying before about St. Ignatius?

Mr. Narrowgate—When there is no evidence of actual mystic life, the militant character comes to the foreground, of course. But the fact of taking part in active life and being successful in it, does not imply that one is primarily an active character. When you say that mysticism is one thing in Spain and another elsewhere in the world, you are thinking of accidentals. The central experience is bound to be the same, as in all the other manifestations of the human soul. A mystic, *qua* mystic, irrespective of his nationality and epoch, must show in himself those three indispensable elements: passivity, obscurity, dispossession. May I now continue with my rapid survey of the Spanish mystics?

Mr. Broadway—Do, *advocatus diaboli*. You will not convince me, though, I warn you.

Mr. Narrowgate—For Alonso de Orozco there is not enough evidence, at least in his writings. I repeat it again: it is not enough to speak of experiences which pass understanding. There is a vocabulary common to all religious writers, and many expressions of that vocabulary have become very early detached from a living experience. As like as not they are mere formulæ. Sometimes you find that your would-be mystic is only quoting from St. Augustine, or even from more recent mystics. Juan de los Ángeles, for instance, is indebted to Ruysbroeck, Tauler, and Gerson, to mention only some of his sources. I will not say that Juan de los Ángeles is no mystic; but his pages sometimes strike me as those of a person who is frightfully learned on his subject, more by reading than by actual experience. The best among those pages not excluded. I am thinking now of famous passages in the first dialogue of his *Conquest of the spiritual and secret Kingdom of God*. Words, as I have said, often convey more than they are entitled to. I feel that this is the case of Luís de Granada, an excellent preacher and a forcible ascetic writer, who can descant on the wonders of nature with no less charm and eloquence than the famous Italian Daniello Bartoli; yes, an excellent preacher, but a mystic? Well, only if you take the word in such a broad sense as nearly to in-clude a Daniello Bartoli, too. There are mystical elements in most of the writers I have been mention-ing, but all is a matter of quantity and intensity. There is a potential poet in most prose writers, without their having any claim to be called poets for all that. It may be only a small measure that is needed to tip the balance on one side rather than on the other, but you cannot do without that *quid divinum* which distinguishes a mystic from a non-mystic author. Would you take the *concetti predica-bili*, the sermon-like flights of Pedro Malón de Chaide for sterling mysticism?

Mr. Broadway—And yet Malón de Chaide has been called "the metaphysician of love."

Mr. Narrowgate—Metaphysician, another mis-used word. But you may well call Malón de Chaide metaphysical in so far as his technique reminds one of the metaphysical school of poetry of the seven-teenth century. In a well-known passage of his *Con-version of the Magdalen* he links the "*Ecce Mulier*," which introduces the Magdalen in St. Luke, to-gether with Pilate's expression, "*Ecce Homo*," and works out such a monumental *concetto* as Donne would not have disdained for one of his sermons.

And what about the lavish use of interrogative and exclamative sentences we find in that *Conversion?* For all his eloquence Pedro Malón de Chaide fails to convince me, while, on the other hand, Bernardino de Laredo and Juan de Ávila fail to persuade me, and for the opposite reason, for their restraint, and their lack of powerful words. There are subjects which lend themselves admirably to rhetorical treat‹ ment, and on the wings of rhetoric one is apt to be carried much further than one at first intended. Take Luís de León's *Names of Christ*——

Mr. Broadway—Surely you are not going to say that Luís de León is not a mystic!

Mr. Narrowgate—Luís de León is a great poet, but no mystic. I take Unamuno's description of him as the best: " A Platonist, an imitator of Horace and Virgil, a spirit in which the Epicurean and Stoic merge in the Christian; fond of peace, quiet, and harmony . . ." He is given by Unamuno as a typical instance of the triumph of humanism over Castilian mysticism. And, don't forget, we have Luís de León's own words. When speaking of the mystics he definitely says: "I must confess with regret that I am not of their number."

Mr. Broadway—Cannot a humanist be a mystic, notwithstanding all his admiration for the Horatian golden rule of moderation and a quiet epicurean life? Is not the *Noche Serena* a mystical poem? If an intui‹

tive or immediate consciousness of the supreme reality as one, eternal and spiritual, forms the very essence of mysticism, as I seem to have read somewhere, how can you deny that Luís de León was a mystic?

Mr. Narrowgate—The *Noche Serena* is a fine poem, but what is the upshot of it? "What misfortune causes my soul to be pent in this low, dark prison of earth?"—says Luís de León—"Life is vanity and deceit. Oh, lift your eyes to the eternal spheres of heaven. Earth is but an insignificant speck . . ." I shall not tell you how easily one could trace these ideas to their Platonic and Petrarchan sources. Let us take them as if they were original. What of that? Is Shelley a mystic because of his *Ode to the West Wind*? Is Wordsworth a mystic because of many noble passages in both the *Prelude* and the *Excursion*? Is Keats a mystic because of his *Ode to a Nightingale*? If you take mysticism to mean an intuitive consciousness of the supreme reality as one, eternal and spiritual, then all great poets, all great artists indeed are entitled to be called mystics. In a sense, every work of art makes you feel the presence of God, tells of his glory. But this is too wide a denominator. Mysticism and art are two different aspects of the same reality, if you like, but they are so different as to be opposite. In a word, the artist's aim is expression, a concrete expression; the mystic's aim, in the words of St. John of the Cross, is a general, obscure contemplation. *Confuso, oscuro, general,* are three adjectives on which St. John particularly insists. The mystic's aim is to get away from all phenomenal representation: *"sin materia de sensitiva recreación."* His supreme confession is the Sanskrit *"Neti, Neti, Neti,"* "It is not that, it is not that, it is not that." None of the expressions which appeal to the senses or to reason is able to convey the mystic's idea of the Divine. The mystic's attitude is " a will founded on the void of faith," according to the powerful definition of St. John: *"voluntad fundada en vacio de fé."* Both the artist and the mystic aim at a Universal. But the artist's idea of the universal is embodied in a clear, well-defined shape; the mystic's idea of the universal is obscure, purposely kept free from any well-defined shape. For all the insistence on the idea of possession of God you find in the Spanish mystics, the mystic's is a receptive attitude. The mystic's aim is to discard all earthly limitations, to create a void in himself, in order *to be shaped* anew by God. The artist's aim is *to shape.* The mystic's rhythm fulfils itself in silence and self-annihilation, but the artist's rhythm is nothing if not expression, self-assertion, sensible Beauty.

Mr. Broadway—But Beauty is also the aim of St. John of the Cross; "Let us do in such way, that by means of this exercise of love we may come to see each other in thy beauty..." You know the sublime passage.

Mr. Narrowgate—Yes, Beauty, but not plastic beauty, rather abstract Beauty; not immanent beauty, transcendent Beauty. A Beauty whose symbol is Night, a Night which is "a deep but dazzling darkness"—to use the words of an English poet, Henry Vaughan. A beauty which is untranslatable into the language of the senses. A thing which is pure and obscure, not felt nor indeed conceived: defying knowledge.

Mr. Broadway—Do you deny then the possibility of a mystic art?

Mr. Narrowgate—Surely, the two things are contradictory. When a mystic expresses himself in a work of art he has ceased to be a mystic. Even music, to which Schopenhauer thought one could assign a position apart——

Mr. Broadway—No, let us take the case of painting. Will you say that El Greco is not a mystic painter? Is not the *Burial of the Count of Orgaz* a perfect expression of Spanish mysticism? Is not the *Christ embracing the Cross*, with his head raised to the sky, his tearful eyes lost in contemplation, a perfect image of the mystic soul? Is not the painting called the *Tears of St. Peter*, in the National Gallery, the pictorial counterpart of the trances described by the mystics? Are not the *Immaculate Conception*

196

and the *Descent of the Holy Ghost* filled with an un⸗
earthly ecstasy? I wish I had here René Schwob's
book on *Profondeurs de l'Espagne* to read you a few
excellent pages about El Greco, and the mystical
character of Spanish painting in general——

Mr. Narrowgate—I have got that book.
Here it is.

Mr. Broadway—What does all this underlining
mean? What those slashes? Honestly, marks would
be too mild a name for them. Oh, you are a thorough
advocatus diaboli. I am afraid your disdain is too
much like the light⸗hearted scorn some people have
of things they cannot understand——

Mr. Narrowgate—I have no contempt for Mr.
Schwob's book. On the contrary, I think there are
good points in it. Mr. Schwob is a fervent soul, "de⸗
voured by a longing for unity": very likely a recent
convert. He cannot help seeing religious allusions
everywhere. He wants leading⸗strings to his new⸗
born faith, I suppose. I dare say you know John
Donne's poem on the *Cross*. The poet sees crosses
everywhere. When I stretch my arms, I make a
cross; when I swim, I make a cross; and so on. Surely
travesty lies that way. French authors are noted for
indulging in this sort of religious pun. You find
something very similar to those conceits of Donne in
Paul Claudel, and in León Bloy too. And in René
Schwob, of course. Let me see—Here we are: page

197

one hundred. The rhythm of the composition of the *Meninas* reminds him of a cross. And do you remember what reason is given for the red colour one finds mixed in the blue of Goya's skies? You would think it probable that Goya had taken it from the eighteenth-century Venetians. But no; that red colour stands for blood: Goya is obsessed by blood because he did not know how to consecrate it. Goya is a miscarried mystic. Goya's use of the colour red in the texture of his skies is "a mystery akin to that which the priest celebrates on the altar." And have you noticed that every work of El Greco is an illustration of the mystery of Trinity? That El Greco may be defined by the figure 3? Velázquez has a way of dealing with figures as if they were tabernacles; the figures of his portraits are, in fact, similar to lit candles. His Bacchus in the *Borrachos* is the soul of wine and perhaps, *singulièrement*, as Mr. Schwob says, of that wine into which divine blood has turned. Oh, indeed Mr. Schwob is right in speaking of the *"mécanique enivrante"* of his mind! But why should one scoff at these and similar vagaries? They are the expression of an earnest desire which tries to satisfy itself as best it can in looking at paintings; but really it seems to me that Mr. Schwob wants to square the circle. The universal that Mr. Schwob can find in paintings is a concrete universal, but he craves for a vague, obscure universal, the

198

mystic's universal. His predilection is for what is formless; to all the paintings in Toledo, a few Grecos excepted, he prefers the traces of frescoes in the little Church of the Cristo de la Luz. They are not works of art; but they have a deep emotional appeal for Mr. Schwob's religious soul. He finds some extremely primitive Iberic sculptures more telling than "the most externally precise of statues, the most perfect masterpieces of the outward likeness," because those primitive stones give him a shock of ancestral recognition, they represent *"l'extase de la matière."* For him, European painting is the *"musique de l'inconscient."* An idea which has the only merits of being obscure and confused. What I chiefly resent in Mr. Schwob is the plethora of such words as *religieux, catholique, liturgique, œcuménique, surnaturel, profondeur, grandeur, hiérarchie, éternité, révélation, extase, essence, spiritualisation, sanctification, sanctifier, purifier, consacrer, intérieur, parabolique, métaphysique,* and last, but not least, *mystique.* Every great art, again, is religious art, but not in the technical sense Mr. Schwob wants to give to it. You may jumble together painters and artsts of all descriptions, as in Baudelaire's *Les Phares,* and say that they substantially deliver the same message, bear witness to the same universal idea. But you cannot strain the point without falling into absurdities; you cannot adopt it for the study of details. If you want the *reductio ad absurdum* of the popular idea of mysticism you could hardly do better than quote Mr. Schwob——

Mr. Broadway—How do you explain then certain features of El Greco's art? Does not a passage like this one I find on page 108 strike you as the result of accurate observation? "Greco's figures are like strayed flames under the thick vault of the clouds; through them a permanent osmosis is achieved between the earth which is disintegrating and the sky which is solidifying." Or this other passage: "All his saints literally seem to die of not dying."

Mr. Narrowgate—All this has already been expounded by Barrès: "*Ses personnages saints ne sont plus que des flammes.*" Barrès said that El Greco's canvases completed the treatises of St. Teresa and the poems of St. John of the Cross. From Barrès's book on El Greco Mr. Schwob has also derived an error, alas, when he imagines that the naked figure at the feet of Christ, in the upper part of the *Burial of the Count of Orgaz*, represents the soul of the Count, whereas that figure has been proved to be St. John the Baptist, the whole group being the *Deësis* of Byzantine iconography——

Mr. Broadway—But listen, do you not really think that El Greco's paintings are a sort of pictorial transposition of Spanish mysticism? What more

EL GRECO   *Photo : Anderson*

The Descent of the Holy Ghost

natural, after all? El Greco must have been steeped in the mysticism of the times——

Mr. Narrowgate—Yes, a transposition, if you like. And I am prepared to admit the same for every work of art, have I not said it? Every work of art confesses to the existence of a supreme reality which is one, eternal and spiritual. Or, to put it in Mr. Schwob's figurative language, *"tout grand art ne serait qu'une incantation cosmique."* But if you want to go further than this, and descend to details, do you know what you will get? Allegorical interpretation, nothing else. For Mr. Schwob Velázquez's portrait of Margaret of Austria is "the plastic transposition of a salute of the Holy Sacrament." And why, please? Because the pale face is surrounded by vaporous masses of shadows, and these masses remind Mr. Schwob of clouds of incense: *"Par une magie semblable à celle qui fait apparaître l'hostie plus blanche, au milieu des nuages de l'encens et des ornements d'or dont l'autel est chargé, ce portrait est la transposition plastique d'un salut du Saint-Sacrement."* So a pale face surrounded by dim shadows is the emblem of the Host. A figure elongated and almost volatilised like those painted by El Greco is the emblem of a mystical aspiration. The figure of Bacchus is the emblem of the wine of the mass, and the omnipresence of blood-red in the paintings of Goya symbolises the unity of the universe. Now,

take any of the emblem-books you see ranged on
that shelf over there, and look into it, and tell me
whether Mr. Schwob is not using exactly the same
kind of language as those fanciful and quaint authors
of the seventeenth century. Take for instance those
delightful *Partheneia Sacra*, the work of an English
Jesuit, or Picinelli's monumental encyclopædia, or
any other you like. Now, what is the use of allegoris-
ing, or, as Mr. Schwob puts it, making a *"commen-
taire métaphysique"* on Spanish painters? What useful purpose, pray, is served by organising Velázquez's works as a congregation of devout personages,
"une assemblée de fidèles," round his Christ? What
does it mean that *"leur juxtaposition donne à son
œuvre un caractère œcuménique,"* beyond a vague
high-sounding expression?

But let us come back to the peculiar transposition
which El Greco's paintings are supposed to represent, beyond that transposition of a general
character which is common to all great works of art.
You say that El Greco was steeped in the mysticism
of the times. A definite, historical conception of life
can be traced in every work of art : there is bound to
be a substratum of culture in every poem, painting,
musical composition, and so on, belonging to a certain period. Byzantine mosaics, Venetian paintings,
Castilian landscape and humanity are among the
elements which we must take into account when we

examine the genesis of El Greco's manner. And Counter-Reformation, too, and mysticism, too. But to say that El Greco's paintings mirror a peculiar society is one thing, and to call him a mystic painter is another. Let us even go so far as to admit that El Greco, when he painted his figures, wanted to con-vey the idea of a mystical aspiration in them. Is the painter of a battle himself a warrior? Need I repeat to you one of the truisms of æsthetics? The central feature of a painter's inspiration is *what he sees*: forms, colours. What falls under the senses, the phenomenal world. Metaphysical painting is a hybrid. Painting is good enough if it is just painting. But a painter, *qua* painter, is the very antithesis of a mystic, as I have already said. El Greco is far from having renounced pleasure, as Mr. Schwob affirms. With a little alteration the words of that Englishman, whom our French author found so dense, sound quite right: "El Greco was never a mystic (the Englishman said: a Christian): the joy he felt in painting a beautiful body proves it." Had El Greco been a mystic, he would have felt what Mr. Schwob says in a moment of passionate confession: "I feel an icono-clast's hatred rising from the bottom of my soul. All these images leave my interrogation unan-swered. Are they nothing else but debasement and sacrilege? Is it possible, o my God, to express you otherwise than in the burning ecstasy of *silence*?

Every gesture is a profanation of the Purity which comprehends them all." Had this been El Greco's feeling, then there would be no paintings of El Greco to speak of.

Let us not make confusions of words. Let us not use an ambiguous vocabulary as Mr. Schwob does—here, on page 104: "Painting is the expression of the tendency of the soul to go out of itself, to discover the most intimate affinities between things; it is precisely a manifestation of our longing for unity." All this can equally well be said of the mystic's experience. But in the painter's case the words must be taken in a sense entirely different from that which they would assume in the religious field. For the painter the process described by Mr. Schwob results in affirming the unity of the universe in a concrete work of art. This is his way of worshipping God: in adhering enthusiastically to the world of the senses. But I need not labour the point; we have Mr. Schwob's words for it—here: *"Une recherche passionnée de l'unité du monde dans ses formes concrètes anima toutes les démarches de la pensée du Greco."* Mr. Schwob lets himself be led astray by words. He sees in the surrounding world only what is his present fixed idea: he sees crosses everywhere. Not all things which present the form of a cross are endowed with a religious import: if you affirm it seriously you perpetrate a pun. And Mr. Schwob perpetrates many a pun with his two favourite words: *métaphysique* and *mystique*.

How many things that ill-starred word "mystic" is forced to cover! I dare say that you have read Sherwood Anderson's novel *Dark Laughter*; a much better book, by the way, than one would anticipate after reading Wyndham Lewis's dissection of it in *Paleface*. But Mr. Lewis is right when he pillories a sentence like this: "Brown *mysticism* in the walls of a room, in the hair—of a Frenchman, in the eyes of a brown girl." As you see, the same word is used for the experience of St. John of the Cross and for a love which consists, as Mr. Anderson says, in "smelling strangeness." If things continue at this rate, you will very soon see the word "mystic" losing caste, and you will not be surprised at finding it some day hobnobbing with lemans, courtesans, banditti, and similar words debased from their original meanings. Do you not think that it would be rather wise to start a Society for the Protection of Words, as somebody has suggested? A penalty not exceeding five pounds should be enforced every time the word "mystic" is improperly used.

Mr. Broadway (rather exhausted, has just enough strength left to yawn a mild pun)—I am afraid in this ca-a-ase Mr. Schwob would not be long in acquiring one of your requisites of sterling mysticism, namely dispossession.

205

EL CAMARÍN

EL CAMARÍN

Cujus est regio, illius et religio

". . . there being a Geography of Religions as well as Lands, and every Clime distinguished not onely by their lawes and limits, but circumscribed by their doctrines and rules of Faith."
—SIR THOMAS BROWNE.

"I looked around for the abominable thing and found it not; no scarlet strumpet with a crown of false gold sat nursing an ugly changeling in a niche."—GEORGE BORROW.

" There are four large pictures of the Conception by Murillo in the Madrid gallery. I spent several mornings in front of those four pictures, motionless, almost entranced. Chiefly the one which is only a fragment ravished me—I was seized by an inex⁄ pressible passion for that face. More than once, while looking at her, I felt tears running down my cheeks. I have never felt so near to faith as in those moments; I have never felt so full of goodwill, and I believe that my soul has never shone brighter in my face."—EDMONDO DE AMICIS.

HERE they are, the Northener and the Southerner, in front of the Madonna. What for the latter is the most exquisite symbol of godhead, awakes only un⁄ pleasant images in the former. They might go on with their discussion until doomsday, and all the most merciless arguments of the fanatic George would fail to convince the tearful Edmondo that his religion is the naïve sublimation of an erotic im⁄

O   209

pulse, while, on the other hand, Edmondo's arguments (supposing he were an argumentative person)
would not persuade George that his sense of repul-
sion in front of a phenomenon so natural as the deifi-
cation of motherhood argues an impurity deeper
than naïve eroticism (but Edmondo ignores Freud,
and would be unable to explain George's attitude as
the result of a repression).

In order to feel full of religious inspiration,
George must think of the God of Battles; the other,
when he wants to feel near to faith, knows no better
than contemplating the beautiful features of a Madonna. Man is made of flesh and blood, and, in
whichsoever way it should please him to conceive
divinity, he cannot do it unless with the means at his
command, i.e. always starting from a human basis;
and no Calvinist ratiocination will ever succeed in
demonstrating that the feeling of warlike excitement
is less objectionable than the feeling of erotic
enthusiasm.

A quarter of an hour of innocent amusement can
be procured by an attempt to scrape the veneer of
advanced culture off the souls of both Borrow and
De Amicis. The result of such a process might be
couched in something similar to E. Giménez Caballero's folkloristic essay on the Virgin.

On the one hand you would see George Borrow in
the garb of a Norse warrior fighting a hopeless battle

desperately, until the forces of evil triumph in the day of Ragnarök; on the other you would have Edmondo De Amicis as Don Juan, who, surfeited in the long run with love-making and easy success, postulates an Impossible She, an unattainable Beloved, as much above him as he has found everyday woman below. In both cases man's career culminates and ends in a defeat: man confesses himself overcome and worships his opponent. The warrior deifies the evil powers against which he has been fighting. Borrow's God represents the last version of Fenris-Wolf, the grim power in which all the hardships of life in a severe climate, first of all hunger, are symbolised; that evil power which shall advance with a gaping mouth,—his lower jaw against the earth, and his upper against heaven—, and shall swallow the sun. The lover, after a vain search on earth for a woman who could not be defiled, projects an ideal image of Femininity into a supernatural world, and surrenders to her. That Conception of Murillo in front of whom De Amicis feels enraptured is the sister of the one painted by the same painter in the Hospital de la Caridad at the command of Don Miguel Mañara, the prototype of Don Juan: that divine woman in the full bloom of her ripeness, *"en su plenitud sexual,"* who treads underfoot Eve's conqueror, the Serpent, and sails through heaven on that pagan symbol of purity, Diana's moon, represents the final stage of Don Juan's libido: the stage of sublimation. Sex on the one hand, Hunger on the other. But hunger and sex are closely related, and you, George Borrow, reviler of the tawdry Whore of Babylon and devotee of the God of the Psalms and Prophecies, you are no such distant relative of the effeminate worshipper you despise. As a matter of fact, with a little juggling trick *à la* Giménez Caballero, you are shown to be substantially the same.

But fortunately Giménez Caballero did not exist in your time, George Borrow; otherwise I would have been very sorry for you. You had thought yourself firmly seated on the top of an ivory tower, able to look with a clear eye into man's base corruption. What would have happened if one of the crowd below, a sceptical Spaniard, Giménez Caballero, had come to the foot of your comfortable erection and whispered: "You might as well come down among us, you know"? What would you have done, George Borrow? Did you by any chance keep a saw at your side, up there in that breezy eminence, so that you could bravely cut down under you your flawless ivory tower?

Once we have admitted that every supernatural conception can be traced to some natural emotion, that every emblem needs a "body," and that a body, exquisite as the choice may happen to be, cannot help being a body, i.e. something material, we shall leave George and Edmondo free to approach the divine through the means which are best suited to appeal to their natures, and present the former with a copy of the Psalms and the Prophets, the latter with an illuminated edition of the Song of Solomon.

After all, the fact that the atmosphere of Spanish churches seems so voluptuous to a foreigner, does not prove that Spaniards necessarily feel it so. Nothing is likelier to be taken as a defect or a sin, than a regional or national peculiarity. English reserve is termed hypocrisy by Continentals, Italian sprightliness is called theatricality by the Teutons, Russian charity strikes an Occidental as weakness of volition —each virtue is turned into its corresponding vice, and from the remotest antiquity such anti-foreign litanies are current as this, which Shirley attributed to Lydgate:

> Subtilis duplicitas Italicorum
> Manifesta luxuria Theothonicorum
> Frentosa duricies Ispanorum
> Effrenata superbia Gallicorum
> Parca fidelitas Anglicorum . . .

A Spaniard will no doubt feel indignant at seeing his Madonna identified with the Whore of Babylon, but will he be aware of what is really implied by such blasphemy? Since, in order to be aware of it, he would have to be capable of such radical introspec-

213

tion as is hardly conceivable in a Southern mind.
Borrow, by spreading his own disgust for the Whore
of Babylon among Spanish peasants, might have
succeeded in weaning them from the cult of images,
but could he have hoped to graft in its place the
habit of self-examination? He himself perceived at
last how, without the necessary preparation, even
the Bible is a book sealed with seven seals; so, how
could he suppose that Spaniards would succeed in
one day in reading the Bible as Englishmen did after
an age-long evolution? The Spaniards, one of the
slowest races! What Borrow propagated in Spain
was not the Bible, but atheism. Either black or red:
there is no middle way for certain races. They must
either conceive the divine in those forms and with
those means which originate in the deep roots of
their racial character, or not conceive it at all, and
deny it. Borrow could turn Spaniards into icono-
clasts, but hardly into protestants. It is easy to
destroy in one hour the work of centuries, but is
there not a monstrous simplicity in attempting to
build in one day what it has required a thousand
years to produce? Besides, is it really true that in one
hour the work of centuries can be annihilated? Certain idiosyncrasies reproduce themselves with the
insistence of the very national characteristics to
which they are peculiar: so long as the race remains
the same, the typical idiosyncrasy will crop up over

and over again in the least expected ways. *Después de años mil, vuelve el rio a su cubil*. Missionaries may boast of having uprooted idolatry from some savage tribe. Sooner or later one finds that the would-be convert conceives Christ as a phallic divinity, or whatnot.

A similar remark could be made in the field of politics, and one may admire indeed the beneficent effects of a constitutional regime in the South American republics, in Portugal, in the Balkans, in China.

"Do you call yourself free? It is your dominant thoughts I want to know, and not how you have shaken off a yoke. Are you such one as needed to shake off a yoke? There are men who lose their last worth, whilst they throw away their servility."

Thus spake Zarathustra.

Therefore let them thrive, those multitudes of mantled and crowned Madonnas who, sometimes rigid in their wooden stupor, sometimes wild with a superhuman sorrow—according to the artist's ability—overlook the congregation from their altars, in the midst of a wilderness of either spangles and gewgaws, or actual jewels and genuine finery.

A Whore of Babylon, she? Never. She is a lady as good as she is beautiful, who has suffered much and is exceedingly compassionate: she is the World's

Queen, Heaven's Queen. So the Spaniard thinks, not only the peasant, but also the grandee. I, for myself, do not know of any more touching evidence of this conception of the Virgin as of a good charit‑able and affable lady, than a certain statue which is to be found in one of the churches of Gerona. Our Lady appears there dressed in crinoline and wearing a cloche hat tied with a velvet bow under her chin; she offers to play with the Child and her gesture is no less graceful than that of an Arcadian shepherdess. Borrow may well call her a strumpet. For the good citizen of Gerona she is Our Blessed Lady of the Heavenly Palace, who does not demur to walk in the public street dressed in the latest fashion, and to bestow on her pretty Child such innocent blandish‑ments as call happy tears to the eyes of good gossips.

In a country where affability among the various classes is spontaneous and traditional (none of your Northern philanthropy, which is often so degrading to the humble!) Heaven's Queen is also a *grande dame* of easy access, "humble and heigh over every creature," she lends a benign ear to the compliments and sobs of the poor folk, and intercedes like the good advocate she is. What can one do for her who has suffered so much and is so compassionate? Gold —think as you may—glitters to the eyes of the humble people "over and above any other magnani‑

mous riches," as Pindar has it; gold is the highest perceivable good, and the people know of no better way of showing their love and gratitude than by heaping gold on Heaven's Queen, from head to foot. And in what else does a bride's greatest wealth lie if not in her trousseau? How could Heaven's Bride be without a trousseau? Therefore she must be supplied with precious mantles stiff with gold embroidery, superfine robes and petticoats, of every sort and colour, according to the various days and seasons. There is the Virgen del Sagrario in Toledo who has been described as the wealthiest match in all Spain; her wardrobe is richer in *robes* and *manteaux* than that of any queen of the world. What is illogical in all this? Babylonian gaudiness, sensuousness of the cult, idolatry: big words. The satisfaction of the devout is not confined to the eye. The eye is merely the straightest way to reach the heart, as the ear is for others, and for others, maybe, reason. The satisfaction of the devout is to know that he has done everything in his power to show his gratitude and to comfort Our Lady of Sorrows, who is so unhappy and so good. Now they have killed her Son, her dead Son lies on her knees, on the knees of the Virgen de las Angustias.

> Donna del Paradiso,
> Lo tuo figliolo è preso,
> Jesù Cristo beato . . .

The spirit of the old heart-rending *lauda* breathes also in the monotonous *saetas* of the humble folk, moved at the sight of the divine anguish. What can humble folk do in order to comfort the Virgin of Sorrows? With certain peoples funerals are still followed by the curious celebration of a feast, in which friends try to entertain the close relatives of the dead as best they can. Surely that feast will not succeed in bringing comfort; still a naïve and awkward goodwill is implied by the name of *riconsolo* given to that ceremony in Calabria. In the same way the humble folk offer to the Virgin what is most precious on earth. A gaudy crown on the head of the Madonna; a stiff, trailing mantle all embroidered with little palms, garlands, roses, drops, pomegranates of gold; on her breast numberless jewels; an enormous silver crescent with her monogram, at her feet; a precious pall on the body of Christ lying on her knees; bundles of rays jutting from behind the cross, so that it appears to be a miraculous palm from which, instead of fruits, hang the gold embroidered ribbons.

How impious—Borrow will say—to think that the Omnipotent needs the ludicrous gewgaws of this world! Of course He does not need them, but blasphemy is not in question. Man is man, and when a child offers to his crying playmate his own toys, in order to console him, does he not act out of sheer kindliness? Why, then, should the same act cease to be a kindly one, when it is accomplished by that grown-up child, man? Excessive anthropomorphism? Still when in the Alameda of Granada I see all the passers-by take off their hats, and often kneel down for a short prayer, in front of the dwelling of the Virgen de las Angustias (since there is no doubt, the Madonna actually dwells inside there), I find that the silent act of homage is not instinct with a superstitious servility, but rather with something more intimate and profound, and I feel that the public thoroughfare is animated by an invisible presence, while I do not feel the same in a protestant church during the ten thousand words of the Sunday sermon.

Not even the camarín behind the high altar succeeds in arousing either my indignation or even my laughter. There is something theatrical in the idea of a *camarín*. In that theatre which is a Catholic church, the *camarín* stands for the stage and the royal loge at the same time, the greenroom where the Virgin's wardrobe is kept, and the throne room. When the show is due, the curtain will rise, and the great actress of the divine drama appear at the balcony of her palace, and glitter like a monstrance. If in Spanish churches they had adopted the baroque device (illustrated in the church of Gesù e Maria in Rome) of building the tombs in the nave in the form of *loges*, at whose parapets the bust effigies of the dead are seen leaning, while they watch the high altar, the illusion would be complete. Is there blasphemy in such a theatrical fiction? Have rite and spectacle not been branches of the same trunk, from the remotest antiquity?

A Southern catholic church is a theatre, a protestant church is a lecture-room; Southern religion is overflow of enthusiasm, Northern religion is persuasion by reasoning: the appearance of the church at once betrays the character of the faith. For my own part I leave to the Northerners the flat homily and, with Thomas Browne, I own to being "naturally inclined to that which misguided zeal terms superstition." I am not even taken aback by the appearance of Sevillian churches on the Thursday before Easter. I prefer the beautiful Sevillian women sitting at the *mesas petitorias*, who make the silver coins ring in the dim light, while the ogling dandies saunter round the bedizened Madonnas illumined by galaxies of wax-candles ; I prefer even the love-signalling between a paternoster and an avemaria, to the busy, frigid passing to and fro in a protestant bazaar, which in no way differs from the profane sale at a Selfridge's or a Woolworth's. I prefer the parish magazines of the South, for all their unctuous stuff (the actual verbal counterpart of the *mantecado del Corazón de Jesús* sold by Spanish confectioners), and their too, too exemplary lives of saints, to certain parish gazettes of the North, where, immediately under the last words of the meek Vicar's letter ("Think on these things—is St. Paul's advice") one reads an advertisement of parochial marmalade made by the Vicar's wife: "MARMALADE: By the time you receive this month's magazine, the Unrivalled Brand will be on sale." I find the atmosphere of a drawing-room less forbidding than that of a shop. I would rather listen to a competition of *saeta* singers, for all the monotony attendant on such a performance, than to such songs of British nonconformist piety as:

> Jesus is my lover,
> I am walking out with him . . .

or:

> O, to be a Baptist,
> And wear a shiny face,
> And not to be a Methodist
> And always fall from grace . . .

or the immortal one called *Telephone to Glory*:

> O what joy is mine,
> I can feel the current
> Moving down the line,
> Built by God the Father
> For his loved alone,
> We may telephone to Glory
> Through this royal telephone!

And yet, I would not condemn these lyrical out-bursts of the North: every land has its own ways, and infinite are the ways of Our Lord.

The only thing I cannot very well countenance in the *camarín* is not that tawdriness of fresco, marble, and precious metal; neither is it that fantastic galaxy of lights arranged in clusters, circles, spirals, which is a refinement on the illumination of the church (the church is a full orchestra, the *camarín* is a quartet, just as in some theatres there is a special hall for chamber music); the thing which annoys me is the superabundance of relics.

There is no end to those relics; they are foiled with marble and gold, all along the walls, so neatly; and the implacable monkish accuracy does not forgo a single label. This sample fair of holy limbs hap-pens to be very disconcerting, not to say absurd. No matter how many miracles some saints may have worked, one has never heard that they ever attri-buted to themselves, just for fun, ten thigh-bones, or three eyes, or forty-two fingers—since one seems to have seen no less than so many limbs of one saint, after visiting a score or two of cathedrals and churches. And, no matter how powerful the gift of language may have been in a few of them, surely their tongues did not possess the alarming length one would obtain by piecing together all the bits one is shown here and there. The naivety of the collec-

tions of relics is only second to that of certain hagio‹
graphies which telescope several lives of different
martyrs, and ascribe, to each of them, all the various
torments, until each is caused to die by the tradi‹
tional one, after having triumphed over all the
others. I would like the golden legends better with‹
out the elephantiasis of reduplication, and, in the
camarín, I do my best to ignore the displays of relics.

No doubt the images of Spanish saints are often
apt to strike one as melodramatic. Saint Hermen‹
gild, as painted by Herrera, in the Prado, is typical.
Not in the least overawed by the fact of his being
received into Heaven, he finds the strength to sing
a romance to the Crucifix, while the angels accom‹
pany his song on their guitars. Not even the famous
St. Anthony by Murillo in Seville Cathedral, whose
head *"se renverse dans un spasme de volupté céleste"*,
to repeat Gautier's apposite remark, is free from
affectation.

A more intense dramatic character, exempt from
academicism, is to be found in the polychrome
statuettes by Alonso Cano and Pedro de Mena. I am
not blind to the fact that, while Murillo is respon‹
sible for the later chocolate‹box pictures of saints, so
the Spanish wood‹sculptures are the archetypes of
that appalling papier‹mâché statuary which has
spread nowadays from France to all the Catholic
churches of the world. Still, for certain statuettes by

Alonso Cano or Pedro de Mena I have a partiality which I am not willing to suppress. One cannot honestly wish to own any of the paintings, by great masters, which have held us spellbound for hours in the famous art galleries. I cannot picture myself as the owner of the *Meninas*, or of Giorgione's *Concert*; the presence of such a painting in my home would humiliate and disturb me. I should no longer feel master of my house, but rather the responsible keeper of a masterpiece. No liberties are allowed towards such guests; I had rather call on them elsewhere, than be on thorns as their host. They are too transcendent for constant companionship. *J'en serais accablé*, my health would be in serious danger. But there are works of art of a less olympic kind, with which it would be extremely pleasant to have an everyday contact. Among these I reckon Fouquet's illuminations and the polychrome statuettes of Spain. Whereas I could not conceive of the theft of a Rembrandt or a Raphael, the lifting of one of the Chantilly illuminations or of the statuettes of the Immaculate Conception and the Virgin with Child, in the sacristy of the Granada Cathedral, is to be included among my criminal possibilities. And, first of all, I would like to possess that wonderful head of the Mater Dolorosa by Juan Martínez Montañéz in the Kaiser Friedrich Museum, with her so intense, though controlled, divine sorrow, which flows

Mater Dolorosa

BY J. MARTÍNEZ MONTAÑÉZ

gently from the most beautiful eyes of a woman that art has ever achieved. All the tragic composure of the Rondanini Medusa is displayed in that Madonna's face, and, at the same time, such a vehemence of sorrow as only the theatrical art of Spain could represent. I can imagine the sculptor, transcended by his own creation, uttering in front of her a prayer not dissimilar to that written by Duccio di Buoninsegna at the foot of his *Maestà*: "*Mater Sancta Dei*—Holy Mother of God, be thou a cause of peace to my country, be thou life to me, since I made you so."

CICADAS AND CASTANETS

CICADAS AND CASTANETS

τεττίγεσσιν ἐοικότες, οἵ τε καθ' ὕλην
δενδρέῳ ἐφεζόμενοι ὄπα λειριόεσσαν ἱεῖσιν.
—*Homeri Il.*, iii. 151–2.

THE umbrellas of those pines, blurred by the halo of heat, in this fiery time of the day, have suddenly become vocal. The vibration of heat now becomes audible in the crepitation of a shrill metallic note that issues from them. As if the spirit of Summer, landing from the flaming skies in the tangle of the pine forest—like a siren ensnared in the reeds ashore —entreated in his strange inhuman threnody for thirst to be slaked, for a lust to be satiated.

And now I am no longer in the pine forests of Viareggio, where I am writing, but in the *pinares* of Alcalá de Guadaira, and that distant monotone which suddenly flares up and as suddenly dies away, to blaze again more fiercely with the unwearying beat of a tongue of brass, is the sound of the casta-nets, now distant, now near, heard on that festal April afternoon.

Cicadas and castanets, tongues of the hot seasons and the hot countries—be you shaken by the little soul of an insect inebriated with sun, or by a woman's

229

soul inebriated with dance and song—you give the same sound: a monotonous sound of sun-smitten skies, of sun-stricken sands.

The harsh, metallic note multiplies, now closer, now looser, like a pang, like the stab of headache in a hot, sleepless summer night.

Castanets and cicadas, sounds that are as sunny and implacable as the whirr of the guitar and the chirp of the cricket are soft and moon-like. A paroxysm of vivid azure, on the one hand, the liquid calm of the silver-shot blue, on the other. Cicadas and castanets, brass instruments; crickets and guitars, silver cymbals.

Monotonous music beneath monotonous skies. Litanies of tongues of brass, litanies of tongues of silver on earth; while in the sky the hours tell their rosary of gold and turquoise by day, of diamonds and lapis-lazuli, by night. Skies as hard as gems, without the mellowness and the tender lures of the veiled opalescent skies which are changeable as the twilight of an aquarium.

It would suit also your hair, o castanet-playing Andalusian girls, that cicada of gold worn in the hair by the Athenian women.

Alcalá de Guadaira, *pintoresco pueblo*, picturesque little town—so they call it in Seville, so I am going to call it, too, for once. Though Gautier has not entered it in the records of Spanish picturesqueness,

SPANISH DANCE AT THE BEGINNING OF LAST CENTURY

230]

the "picturesque" abounds in the white African*
like town lying by the pine*wooded hills of the
Guadaira. Forgotten there by the Moors in their
flight, a beautiful pearl in that necklace of Arab
settlements which lay scattered all over the usurped
land, when the thread snapped asunder for ever.
Sevilla has the Giralda, Cordoba has the *Mezquita*,
Granada has the Alhambra (do you remember
Victor Hugo's refrain?), Alcalá has nothing; but,
perhaps, it is the most Moorish of them all.

How many times have I looked on it, at noontide,
from the ruins of the Arab castle; how many times
beneath the Passion full moon, from the precincts of
Nuestra Señora del Águila! It was sweet to listen to
the somnolent buzz of innumerable flies in the
spring meadows which submerge relics of the castle
under their teeming life, or to the shrieks of swoop*
ing hawks (sometimes, from a broken tower over my
head, their screech would peal up of a sudden, soon
lost in a whirling of wings like propellers rapidly
spinning ahead); it was sweet, by night, to listen to
the dogs barking here and there from among peace*
ful houses white in the moonlight.

The façade of Nuestra Señora del Águila was my
sun*dial, and only in order to see a shadow stretch its
finger along the white wall glazed with the green
reflection of the underlying meadows, like the mar*
moreal edge of a pond, only in order to see the

231

shadow mark the slow, lazy hours, would you deserve
a pilgrimage, o little Church of Nuestra Señora de
Águila, rich in indulgences. For you can also read
on the façade :

"Esta Iglesia de Nª. Sª. del Águila está unida a la de
Sⁿ Juan de Latrán de Roma y se ganan visitándola
innumerábiles indulgencias; y estando cerrada se
ganan las mismas rezando en esta puerta, laus Deo."

And perhaps those unnumbered indulgences are
secured by the mere act of contemplating the façade,
as I did—which is also a prayer of a kind. Innumerable indulgences! *Aquí, en este país, hay soluciones
para todo.* A Christian church on the ruins of a
Moorish castle, like a flower on its roots. From afar,
as in a mirage, the Saviour on the cornice of St. John
of Lateran raises his blessing hand. He is blessing
that expanse of land which stretches beyond the
walls of Aurelianus—white houses, and the wilderness of the Campagna streaked by the dust trails as
by the passing of caravans; he is blessing this Afri-
can-like country, where the pine is also sovereign,
and where the soil is red and the roads white; and the
houses are white, with terraces instead of roofs.

While spending a morning alone in the green precincts of Nuestra Señora del Águila, there were
moments when I felt my spirit so disposed, that I

wondered whether by repeating three times "*Veni, Sancte Spiritus*," I should have found myself suddenly filled with divine science. People are said to have experienced this after uttering that invocation on their knees, in a solitary field or in a lonely hermitage. But I was disinclined to take the risks of such an experiment—of being assaulted by demons, draggled on land or water, and stricken with an incurable disease: such misfortunes are predicted to the unsuccessful adept by the most reverend Master Ciruelo, who wrote on the magic art in Salamanca, in ages of old. A less ambitious scheme seemed less open to unpleasant surprises.

Methinks I should have liked to have with me at a feast picturesque Théophile Gautier, and tearful Edmondo De Amicis, and also, why not? deliquescent Maurice Barrès and fanatic George Borrow, and see them all in peace and harmony touch glasses, in that plenary indulgence of nature and season. You would have pinned two or three picturesque adjectives onto the landscape, Théo; you would have shed idle tears, Edmondo, and you, George, vented a glorious curse against the wicked Whore; and who knows what abstruse dalliances you would have dreamed, Maurice, for the castanet players (since at Alcalá I have come across real castanet-players, who were no variety artists hired for the use of foreigners); and I should have found nothing amiss, there, under the pines of the *pinares*, amidst the songs, the rockets, and the merry-making of the Andalusian *fiesta*.

For without expecting it or deserving it, I, a scoffer at the picturesque, found myself in the midst of an Andalusian holiday, in the *bella ciudad de los paisajes*, Alcalá de Guadaira. I mixed with the guests, I was one of them in front of the photographers' cameras; I had the pleasure of seeing my likeness reproduced in the *Noticero Sevillano*. Dear Doris, I know you are envying me this piece of luck, to which perhaps you were more entitled than I (you, who accept as gospel truth every legend of Spanish picturesque-ness); but, as you know, it is upon the most hardened sinners that God delights most in bestowing his grace. For me the grace, for you the account of it, if I may be granted your attention!

¡Qué bonito es Alcalá! As the Sevillian religious processions and functions had palled on me, I re-solved on the Saturday before Easter Day to stay in Alcalá and to ramble among the pine woods instead of taking, as usual, the afternoon 'bus to the metro-polis. Perhaps I would write a description of the famous Week to Doris, who had longed so much to see it. But I had no sooner crossed the bridge, than I met troops of people climbing the pine-clad hill with me, while the top was already fairly crowded. They leaned on the parapets of the little belvederes

dotted along the ascent, they were sitting in front of
the chapel, above there, they swarmed down the
grassy slopes; some of them were on horseback, and
some had come by motors. Then I understood why
the conductor had asked me whether I was one of the
guests when he gave me the ticket on the 'bus in
which I had left Seville in the morning. For near
the Torre del Oro the vehicle had been boarded by
a group of Andalusian youths dressed in Sunday
best, black clothes, Cordoban felt hats brushed up
and shining, linen spotless, as befitted a ceremony.
They talked busily, they handed to each other pic⟋
tures of Alcalá: their mood was the lyric mood of
solicitors on holiday.

I recognised some of them sitting at the tables
spread on the top of the hill, under the pines, in front
of the little white town sloping down to the Guadaira
—terraces behind terraces with the fronds of some
palm, here and there, to give the finishing touch to
that Eastern landscape. The *espléndido almuerzo* was
nearly over. The guests, boisterous and shiny
thanks to the abundant food and the balsamic air,
exhaled the smoke of spicy *habanos* from their
nostrils, exuded optimism from all their pores.
Lolling on the chairs, in order to let the food slope
down along a perfect inclined plane, they did not
feel overwhelmed by the fourfold ring of people who
hung over the tables in order to stare with rustic

astonishment at the local notables and the South-
American guests (since the *fiesta* was in honour of
some overseas personages who had assembled in
Seville on Señor Franco's return from the Madrid–
Manila flight). It must have been pretty hot inside
the ring, but, though they frequently mopped their
brows, the banqueters seemed cheerful and breezy,
ready to welcome the speeches.

And now there is a hush, and one of the Authorities gets to his feet (shouts: *¡El alcalde! ¡El alcalde!*)
and reads a few *cuartillas*, in which he brilliantly re-
hearses the virtues of the Race, and lavishes expressions of exalted love, *exaltado amor*, on the beauties
of Alcalá. He rounds off with a winged toast to the
Hispano-American brotherhood, while cheers
crown his raised cup. Next to speak is a portly
gentleman, no doubt a *culto letrado*, a lawyer—one
may guess from the rotundity of his *bellos parrafos* in
praise of the *ciudad de los paisajes*. Sweeping is his
gesture, sure and dignified his elocution, his style is
Asiatic: he exalts the *alcalde* as a paragon citizen, he
exalts an illustrious American visitor as a paragon
architect (the architect beams with delight, the
smoke of his cigar puffs up in little thick clouds, as if
to give evidence of the beat of the heart); finally he
proposes the toast of Spain and the Hispano-American nations; and cheers crown his raised cup. Next
rises a flying-officer. At his full height he reaches the

heads of those sitting around : he is as dark as a grain
of pepper, cocky, with jet-black eyes. He exalts the
glories of the Iberic Race *vibrantemente*, he finds
frases de elevados conceptos for the architect "who has
brought to us the embrace of Argentine, our
younger sister" (thicker and thicker the smoke of
the cigar puffs up, the cigar-tip glows, the point of
the architect's nose glows, at intervals, like a light-
house). The bird-like officer squares his chest, and
speaks of *explosión de la emoción*, of *fervor de nuestro
espíritu*, of the modest contribution to the Hispano-
American brotherhood made by himself, a distant son of that Cristóbal Colón who was born in
Galicia, as all Spaniards know, though History
knows it otherwise. And cheers crown *his* raised
cup. Next stands up a suburban reporter, *culto y
prestijioso letrado*, and reads with volcanic vigour some
admirable *cuartillas*, in which nothing is forgotten :
neither the beauties of Alcalá, nor the high destinies
of the Race, one of whose admirable offsprings, the
Architect, "can say loud and proudly that he came
and conquered." And cheers crown *his* raised cup.
We regret the scantiness of space which prevents us
from reproducing *tan bello trabajo* as well as the two
or three following speeches; but I can assure you
that none, absolutely none, of the speakers forgot to
descant upon the lofty destinies of the Race, the
spiritual *entente* between Spain and America, *el*

fervor de la emoción, the gratitude of the Country, justly proud of such children, and the feats of the Argentine Architect. At last, crowned with smoke as if with clouds, amidst a thunder of cheers, he stands up, the great man, the worthy son of Iberia, the illustrious Architect, the big pot. After so many rockets of elocution, his speech is the flower-bomb, the Catherine-wheel, the final grand salvo, destined to carry the crowd off their feet. He also begins by exalting the beautiful landscape, and the art of all the Andalusian peoples, he welcomes the praises addressed to himself as being directed to his own Country (*cheers*). He says that the time has come when all the Spanish-speaking nations must assume *personalidad estética* (*loud cheers*), and concludes his short but pithy address with a lyric tribute to the victories in the air, to the *triunfante expedición*, the *enorme actuación*, the *júbilo del corazón*, the *simpática manifestación*, his own *muy grande satisfacción*, the universal *espiritual compenetración*. At the end of his speech, the illustrious Architect reaps a *nutrida ovación*.

The cheerful faces oozed with sweat. As in the ceiling of a baroque church stout, plump, and ruddy sit the enthroned saints, so round the tables sat the flushed guests. And on the tables swarms of flies assaulted the relics of the feast, the half-empty glasses, the napkins tattooed with the kisses of juicy lips;

while from among the pines bundles of sunbeams darted in all directions, as from stucco clouds dart glories of golden plaster. Such a glorious moment needed Luca Giordano's brush to record it, rather than the cameras of photographers, professionals and amateurs, clicking here and there, during the concluding phases.

There is a quality of stiffness and starchiness about the official dinners of the Latin countries, which cannot be fully relished until one has experienced the other extreme, an English banquet. Here no sooner has the King's health been proposed with all the concentration and hush attending such toast, than a spell of distension takes place. The elbows relax into a freer play, the voices, as if cleared by the glass of port, indulge the full scale of their modulations; lounging attitudes accompany the permission to smoke; the way is royally paved for the appearance of the fairy guest who wears his silk hat askew over a genial face and sways in his hand the sceptre tingling with silver bells: WIT. As if one could not name the King, without releasing his inseparable companion, the Jester. Wit is a graceful, informal ruler, but a terribly exacting one. There is no sullen, morose, unclubbable guest who does not feel a gentleman's duty to turn to his neighbour with an ingratiating smile and a genial remark, possibly a humorous one. Wit's tyranny is the sweetest of

tyrannies; he binds with rose garlands, he knows
Elagabalus's trick of smothering his subjects in
flowers: "*oppressit violis et floribus.*" He is

The implacable beautiful tyrant,
Rose-crowned, having death in his hands.

Woe to the speaker who does not know how to inter-
sperse his after-dinner address with opportune solici-
tations to Wit's attendant, Laughter; woe to him at
whose solicitation the fairy guest refuses to shake his
tingling sceptre in sign of merriment. I have seen
strong, gifted men "draw bitter and perilous breath"
at the idea of such a failure, who would have faced
without blinking the aspect of a full Court, and even
the rifles of the enemy. Personal merits, remarkable
achievements, a career of well-deserving work, little
avail, if you prove a dull speaker, a bore. Wit's hand
is a gentle hand, prettily manicured, but its down-
cast thumb is more ominous than Cæsar's. At an
English banquet you are expected to produce jokes,
to be witty, you must smile while dancing on hot
coals, and distort your smarting face into a grin as
near as possible to a smile. Better laugh yourself ex-
tinct "as if you had swallow'd a pound of saffron,"
better die, with a tarantula, dancing and singing,
than disgrace yourself by the odious reputation of a
dull person, a kill-joy, a bore. Since the presence of

a bore is no less avoided in England than, in the South of Europe, that of a *iettatore*.

But Wit's dominion hardly reaches South of the Channel. The Jester vainly knocks at the doors of the Latin banqueting halls. He is left in the outer darkness, with his extinguished lamp, like one of the foolish virgins. Merry are the streets and cafés of the Latin countries, but the official banquets are as solemn as funerals. No matter how jovial you are in ordinary life: when you deliver an after-dinner address there, you must divest yourself of all gay colours, and put on ceremonial robes. You are expected to voice the Soul of the Race, you wear on your forehead a Sanbenito stamped with the Declaration of the *Droits de l'Homme*, or the High Destinies of the Imperial Race; your voice must soar high and rumble like thunder, and, no matter what you say, you will take care to let the climax of your lofty sentences rest on such words as suggest power, devotion, heroism, which will never cloy your fellow-guests. You are for a moment a Pindar in duodecimo, rattling off dreary genealogies of heroes, without as much as a qualm. Here a condescension to Wit might be fatal indeed; you might earn the renown of a trifler, a scoffer, a man "fit for treasons, stratagems and spoils." For all this, one is rather surprised to hear that momentous transactions are often concluded in England over a glass of port, between two jokes, while in most cases the Latin surge of oratory spouted forth on some gaudy day soon fizzles out like the froth of champagne.

As Heaven would have it, at last they rose from their seats, the Spaniards, and, with the *alcalde* at their head, they proceeded in a body to walk through that beauty, *"a pasear por aquella hermosura, respirando a pleno pulmón aire puro,"* breathing the pure air with expanded lungs. The performance looked somewhat of an exertion, though. They would stumble on the roots of the trees and slip on the fallen pine-needles; and all the way they hardly ceased fanning their liberally perspiring faces with handkerchiefs displayed. Clumsy in their dark Sunday best, haloed by their broad-brimmed Cordoban hats, the worthy sons of Spain waddled on the uneven ground—a grotesque procession of scarecrows and guys, so out of tune in that landscape they had celebrated! The rear was formed by a policeman pushing his bicycle, and the municipal dog-catcher. The policeman's cocked hat, covered with shiny oil-cloth, imitated successfully the black glossy shell of a cockroach. "The *alcalde* made a wonderfully happy speech—*un discurso maravilloso, fortunatísimo"*— said one. Another praised the *sugestivo aspecto* of the landscape.

Indeed nothing could be more beautiful than that scenery, billowy umbrellas of pines, as far as the

242

eye could reach, basking in the sun. And on the ridges chiselled against the loveliest blue, and in every grassy dell as smooth and delicate as a parrot's breast, under the shadow of the numberless pine-trees, the country folk were sitting to picnic and sing. Children were romping here and there, young men dressed in the Andalusian *traje*—Cordoban hat, *bolero*, and leathers (*zahones*)—scoured about on the back of frisky little black horses, some carrying on pillion a *linda muchacha*, or a *guapa mujer*, with either a jasmin or a rose or a carnation in her hair. (Doris, your eyes do sparkle with excitement, now! This, this is the picturesque Spain you find so wonderful in the picture cards, or in those coloured papier-mâché statuettes I have brought you from Seville. Now you look at me with the eyes of Mignon, home-sick for the land where the orange blooms. I know you look at me with such tender eyes only because, this moment, I who am talking to you stand for Spain, I stand for all those beautiful distant things— not because I am I, not for this, of course.)

Riders galloped along the crests of the hills, among the colonnaded alleys of pines, with white Alcalá for a background, Alcalá so white yonder, in full sun-shine, against the clear turquoise sky. The *culto letrado* praised *el pintoresco sitio*, "a wonderful corner superior in charm to whatever could be imagined." Now three, four motor-cars fought their way uphill,

jolting. *"¡Las señoras! ¡Las señoritas!"*—shouted
with outstretched arms the scarecrows and guys,
halting on the summit of a slope, to wait with faces
fixed in an ecstatic smile. Now the ladies alight, ac-
companied by a few obsequious youths. Most of the
ladies have a curious exotic, international appearance: the skirts and belts suggest Broadway, the hats
Rue Saint-Honoré, some wear jerseys made in England. This one is as fair as a Norwegian, that one
there looks Italian, but decidedly the third one is
half-bred; all of them have the typical gait of Spanish
women, little accustomed to walk among roots of
trees and along grassy slopes. Argentine ladies. The
dark men bow, one and all, they luxuriate in profuse
compliments, place themselves *a los pies*. Smiles.
Handkissing. More smiles. Endearments to a little
girl who is likely to *"hacer daño a fuerza de bonita"*—
as runs the *alcalde's* gallant remark apropos of this
fatal beauty in the bud. The walk is resumed.
Oromana is the watchword. To Oromana! To
Oromana! The *alcalde*, with the bravest ones, boldly
breasts a gentle ascent and disappears. The others
straggle behind. Lastly, leaning on the arm of the
culto letrado, comes an old lady whose most adequate
manner of locomotion would be to lie down and
roll herself downhill like a hedgehog, so dumpy and
round is she.

Suddenly, behind us, among the pines, there rose

a tumultuous chirping as of cicadas. It was a fast crackling sound which stopped short with a snap. From the distance, another similar clicking of metallic tongues replied, reached a climax, went out, also, in a moment. Now they crackled here, there, from several sides, as if distilled by the force of the sun, those songs of strange cicadas: as resin is distilled out of the trunks of the pines. It was a con﹐ flagration of sound. Suddenly it went out. Then it started again, and now was speeding up in our direc﹐ tion, mixed with human voices; and now on the near sky﹐line a company of peasant girls appeared, and, in their midst, the dancers, face to face, with upraised canorous arms. ¡Las castañuelas! (The castanets, Doris, those very same shiny castanets which you keep hanging by your mantelpiece and are content to cherish with your eyes, being unable to shake them in your hands. Does it not seem to you, sometimes, as if those hushed musical things, hanging in that corner of a sitting﹐room which re﹐ ceives more light from the fireplace than from the weak English sun, would pine like swallows im﹐ prisoned in a cage? Notwithstanding your beautiful eyes to cherish them, Doris.)

They sang and danced *seguidillas* in honour of the overseas guests, the *bellas muchachas del pueblo.* Beautiful?—they were not really good﹐looking: to none of them the Andalusian epithet of *salada* would have been suited. None of them possessed *salero*; they were village beauties, dowdy and rather thick-set; still, they had a dash of Oriental charm discernible in the glossy dark hair, the dark soft eyes, the slightly aquiline nose, the full lips, the date-coloured skin. And, I must confess, their dancing was a little heavy: there was nothing about it of the nimbleness of the sham Andalusian dancers the tourist admires in Barcelona, in the *cabaret* called Villarosa, or in the *moulins* of Montmartre. Besides, they were rather shy, those girls. "Now you sing." "No, you begin." They blushed, hesitated, felt overawed by the foreign ladies who, with protracted smiles, had stopped to watch, leaning against the pine-trunks. Then suddenly one of the girls, with a wild flash in her eyes, shook the castanets, and started one of those *coplas*, plaintive and at the same time so swift, monotonous as the song of a canary, soaring through the usual progression of singsong, up to the final snap, sudden, unexpected—and the song went out as would a torch dipped into water; the dance stopped; the spell was broken with the last beat of the castanets.

> El dia que tu naciste
> Nacieron todas las flores . . .

Put again that record on the gramophone, Doris, and once again listen to that plaintive, passionate

Photo : *The Times*

SPANISH DANCES TO∂DAY

246]

song which brings so much sun into your wintry
sitting-room, and imagine that those fir-trees in the
garden are the *pinares*; with your chin resting on the
palms of your hands, and with intent gaze, listen to
the first whirr of the record, with a wistful smile
accompany the sudden surprise of the last note,
suspended in the silence:

> Como las zarzamoras
> Por los vallados.]

The other girls around clapped their hands,
rhythmically. Then the ring broke, and the shy
country girls ran down a slope, to begin again their
singing and dancing a little further on. So they
followed us to Oromana, running and rollicking
among the pines. And the awkward bourgeois of
the party did their best to avoid slipping on the pine-
needles, and to hide their embarrassment with
forced smiles. There was a moment when some of
them, near me, felt somehow that they were not
going in the right direction. "Oromana—which
way to Oromana?"—I was asked by a corpulent
youth with conspicuous side-whiskers and a Cordoban hat, who, though out of breath from helping an
Argentine lady up a slope and striving to scramble
up himself, managed to say nice things to her all
the time.

But it was ioye for to seen him swete!

247

"*No se sabe*,"—was my reply. On the top of the hillock another Argentine lady groped for her husband's arm, while her feet refused to proceed, stock-still as a mule's. "*Juanito, ¿no precipitaremos en el abismo? ¡Vuelve luego! . . .*" And with eyes dilated by an adorable agony, she gazed now at the slanting path—the abysm—now at Juanito who was attempting to crawl down with a wary, oblique gait as of a dragged calf. (Do you smile, Doris? I know you are as nimble as a roe on the mountains, like all your countrywomen.) Now also the *culto letrado* with the old lady leaning on his arm reached the top. He breathed freely and evidently thought not a little of his feat, since, after having gazed at the slope below as if from a peak in Darien, he encouraged that lady frightened by the abyss: "*¡A Oromana, señora! ¡A Oromana! ¡Está en el programa!*" As for the old woman, she felt very sorry for herself. "*¡Ahi de mi!*" —she sobbed—"*¡Tengo pierna de Semana Santa!*" Her Holy-Week legs refused to carry her farther. A peasant came our way, and showed us the path to Oromana.

Oromana is a wooded rocky nook at the foot of the hill, on the bank of the river that glides by among the reeds. A fragrance of jasmin hovers about the place, and there is a little uncovered aqueduct, whose pure waters the peasant scoops with a coarse tumbler and offers you with a regal gesture. You drink, if you feel thirsty, and even if you are not athirst you take the tumbler to your lips, such is the kindliness shown in offering you the drink. What does it matter if from the same glass the other guests have drunk? They now sit round on the wall of con-crete or on the moss-grown rocks and watch the dancing and singing which the peasant girls, come down to the river by a short cut, have taken up again here with renewed zest, among the ¡ole! and the sound of clapped hands. But I could do no better than relate the episode in the spirited style of the Sevillian reporter : [1]

"En Oromana, pintoresca finca que está enclavada en el corazón del pinar—en ese pinar donde según Alvárez de Alba, el santero de la ermita se entratiene en torcer los pinos para no aburrirse—, bebimos agua en el mismo manantial donde tienen *su casa* las ranas y cuya agua nos supo a gloria; vimos bailar a unas muchachas, cogimos unas rosas que olían a gloria, chicoleamos a unas jóvenes muy guapas."

[1] In Oromana, a picturesque farm wedged in the heart of the pine forest—in that pine forest where, according to Alvárez de Alba, the anchorite of the hermitage applies himself to twisting the pines in order to avoid getting bored—we drank water in that same source which is the frogs' natural home, a water of a glorious taste; we saw a few girls dance, we plucked a few roses which had a glorious perfume, and we made love to some beautiful young ladies.

The roses had faded a little in the hot noon, the dances were mediocre, the rustic dancers rather overawed by that party of important people sitting round, so that an invitation addressed to them by the gallant corpulent youth, to dance with the gentlemen, was refused with fear (just imagine the tragedy, once the dance were over, if the clownish sweethearts, who surely were those wild youths watching apart, from the bushes yonder, had seen them dance with the strangers!)—certainly that little *fiesta*, taken all in all, was not so delightfully picturesque as you imagine, Doris. However, need I repeat it? perfect picturesqueness exists only in the oleographs, in the *cabarets*, in the descriptions of imaginary travellers, because there the strange exotic elements are wrenched from their vital sod, and distilled into a formula, whereas in real life they are intermixed with so many other human, universal elements which are common to all peoples in all climates. Such picturesque vistas of countries and customs as you find in Paul Morand will never fall under your eyes: you will never see a Negro, wearing a top hat, fish with a bow and arrows, neither will you find that in Siam the unweaned babies delight in smoking cigars. Therefore do not expect real Andalusia to correspond exactly to the Andalusia of the variety stage.

Still, one felt some relief in discovering at Alcalá

de Guadaira how real life, for once, imitated with a sufficient degree of approximation the lively picture of fantasy. We made our way back along the river, we visited a primitive mill, the "classic" mill of El Algarrobo, we trudged up a winding path, and finally we emerged again on the summit, near the chapel, where the tables were still encumbered with the relics of the banquet, and there still stood the dusty motor-cars. Now they had suspended swings from the trunks of the pines, while under the shadow of the numberless trees town and village people were sitting to picnic and sing. The shadows of the pine-trees crept farther, now, but the songs were the same, and everything, even to the position of the groups, seemed the same as before. Some girls vied in sing-ing *saetas*, but most of them rocked themselves in the swings, with skirts tied under the knee. It was the *fiesta del columpio*, which proved *animadísima* thanks to the *numerosas y gentiles muchachas* who took part in it. For the Sevillian reporter that swing festival was similar to many others: very lively, of course, and the girls, needless to say, numerous and comely. To me who, perhaps, shall still see many a girl on a swing, but no longer at Alcalá de Guadaira, that festival was unique.

Presently the crowd would disperse, and the last songs dwindle away in the rosy haze of the sunset, and I should remain there alone—since I had no intention of following the others to the *becerrada*, or to see the feats of the *mancornadores de novillitos* in the *placita* of the little town, neither did I care to watch Señor Epifanio handle the *muleta* (¡*Que bien torea de muleta este chaval!*)—I should remain alone there, to wonder whether the recent spectacle had been a dream of my fantasy, and that stretch of pine-clad country, bordering upon the sky, first a magenta, then a beryl tinged sky, was really Spain, romantic Spain, or, rather, a more familiar landscape, the pine woods of Val di Pesa, for instance.

I am sure you would like to visit Alcalá de Guadaira, dear Doris. And, perhaps, to live there in the pine forest, in sight of the *pintoresco pueblo*, as white as an Arab town, with the fronds of the palms jutting from among the terraces, as if to give colour to that *soupçon* of the East. Perhaps you would love to live in the little *fonda*, if the bed were only a little less forbidding, and "good morning" would sound to you as a new thing, from the full lips of the little servant-maid with coquettish black eyes (a little minx, that maid: she knows how pearls suit her swarthy complexion, so she is very proud of her false ones); and food would seem to you more enjoyable when seasoned by the talk of Antonio, the young Andalusian waiter, intelligent and courteous, really wasted there in the rustic *fonda*, to attend to native yokels and suburban travellers. By the way,

INTERIOR OF A SPANISH INN AT THE BEGINNING OF LAST CENTURY

252]

perhaps you may find Antonio in London, sooner or later, in one of your visits to the Spanish Restaurant in Soho. Since while you, perhaps, would like to live in Alcalá for ever, Antonio is racking his brains how to get out of it as soon as possible. Antonio is fed up with Alcalá, and dreams of Paris and London as the *conquistadores* dreamed of Cipango, Ophir, Eldorado. Yes, even a London fog is apt to appear as a fragment of paradise to the clever *muchacho*. Antonio is intelligent and wants to make money; he does not want to wait on his thrifty countrymen, but to *americanos é ingleses*, who are so generous, or at least this Alcalareño is pleased to think so. Life, for those who have to earn it, is no picturesque adventure. In Antonio's vocabulary Alcalá means drudgery, London means money. In yours, Doris, London stands for dullness, Alcalá for picturesqueness. When Antonio became aware that I was really leaving, that I could not take him with me to happy England (I was a foreigner, and therefore a rich man who could afford to have servants, could I not?), he looked very, very sad. I still see him in the doorway of the *fonda*, in his white jacket, his fine intelligent eyes dimmed with tears (not for me, of course, but for London), while he waves me good-bye: "*Adiós por la vida, ¡Don Mario!*"

FOREIGN WORDS AND PHRASES

A translation of the foreign words and phrases whose meaning is not made clear in the text. No translation is given of the French quotations or of the phrases and words in current use.

PAGE

19. *Per comodidad de sus amigos patrón:* master of the house for the convenience of his friends; *casticísima:* whatever is racy is called *castizo* by the Spaniards.

27. *muchacho:* lad.

29. *¡Me voy a Francia!:* I'll go to France!

35. motto: Nothing new, nothing various, nothing one would wish to see twice.

36. *dolce color d'oriental zaffiro* (Dante): a lovely colour of oriental sapphire.

38. *sin materia de sensitiva recreación* (St. John of the Cross): without anything to stimulate the senses.

44. *desnudez de espíritu* (St. John of the Cross): nakedness of spirit.

49. *paella valenciana:* a Spanish (Valencian) dish of dry rice with meat or chicken, vegetables, etc.

50. *puchero:* a dish of boiled meat and vegetables, a kind of stew; *chuletas de cerdo (de ternero):* pork (veal) cutlets; *bacalao:* codfish; *huevos fritos:* fried eggs; *tortillas:* omelettes; *Entre los pucheros anda el Señor:* Our Lord makes his presence felt amongst the cooking pots; *lucha por garbanzos:* struggle for chick peas (corresponding to English: bread and butter).

52. *piropos:* extravagant compliments, endearing expressions; *aguadores:* water vendors; *gaseosa:* soda water.

58. *¡No hay chinches!:* There are no bugs (in the chairs).

61. *aficionados:* bull-fight amateurs.

65. *And dan he fall down go boom!:* the refrain of a music-hall song popular in Chicago.

66. *mañana:* to-morrow.

67. *¡Echarse al redondel!:* Let's go down to the ring!

68. *descabellar:* to kill the bull by pricking him in the back of the neck with the sword.

69. *¡Fué mucha corridita!:* It was a really paltry corrida!

70. *banderillas de fuego:* banderillas fitted with a rocket which explodes once fixed on the bull's shoulder; *perros:* dogs that are set at the bull to madden him.

73. motto: Were you at least as perfect as animals are! But to animals belongs innocence.

74. *quid divinum:* something divine; *parentesco de dorados:* relationship of gold attires.

75. *seria como fiesta en patio de sacramental:* as serious as a mystery-play.

77. *Qui plus castigat,* etc.: those who chastise most, bind most with love.

82. *El arte de los toros bajó del cielo:* The art of bull-fighting came down from heaven.

88. *reja:* the iron railing in front of the altar.

90. *Katzenjammer:* intoxication; *asqueroso:* nauseous.

91. *Nihil quod tetigit,* etc.: He touched nothing without polluting it.

98. *guia emocional:* emotional guide.

116. *se pasment vint millier:* twenty thousand fall a-swooning.

121. *ords lictz tout grenouillans de punaises:* foul beds all swarming with bugs.

125. *Lo siento mucho:* I am very sorry; *salero:* piquancy.

128. *Que quiere usted,* etc.: What do you want?—My purse, sir, my purse.

132. *Oiga, mujer,* etc.: Listen, woman, is this the way down to the Parral? . . . God save you, and let there be no (unpleasant) news. (A courteous formula.)

136. *Una perrita,* etc.: A penny, sir, give me a penny!

139. *Italia es un país muy bonito:* Italy is a very fine country.

145. *Pero no oigo bien*, etc.: I don't hear well, though. I am eighty years old, sir. I hear very badly; *¡Me gustaba mucho!:* I was hugely pleased with it.

146. *Viva la guardia*, etc.: Long live the police corps, because it is the pride of Spain!

148. *Potius mori quam foedari:* Rather die than be sullied.

155. *Arden claveles*, etc. (Quevedo): Carnations are ablaze in your bright casement, like blazing blood, like splendid wounds.

160. *Hermanos de mi alma*, etc.: brethren of my soul, brethren of my heart; *joyas místicas*, etc.: mystic joys, wisdom of contemplation, pleasure, suavity and delight, exceed﹣ing beauty.

161. *príncipe*, etc.: the prince of our orators, the orator by antonomasia.

165. *capirotes:* conical hats; *Finis Gloriae Mundi*, etc.: The end of worldly glory, The way of all flesh, The sport of death, There is nobody I spare, It makes all things equal.

166. *Aeternitas*, etc.: Eternity, a new process for preserving and embalming corpses, without any surgical inter﹣vention, without undressing the corpse, respecting its sacred inviolability. PRICES: Current outfit, letter A, etc.

167. *Cuidado . . . ¡No me gusta volcar!:* Take care . . . I don't want to be upset.

169. *Navarro dominicano*, etc.: a Dominican of Navarre, a very holy bishop, a man illustrious for his birth, life, doc﹣trine, eloquence, and charity, whose soul was modest in prosperity, steady in adversity, died . . , he expects to put on his immortal self at the sound of the Arch﹣angel's trumpet.

173. *onzas:* doubloons.

177. motto: Many are the thyrsus﹣bearers, but the real Bac﹣chants are few.

192. *concetti predicabili: concetti* suitable for sermons.

215. *Después de años mil*, etc.: After a thousand years, the stream flows back into its bed.

217. *Donna del Paradiso*, etc. (Iacopone da Todi): Lady of Heaven, thy Son is taken prisoner, our blessed Lord Jesus Christ.

229. motto: Like unto cicadas that in a forest sit upon a tree and pour forth their lily-like voice.

232. *Aquí, en este país*, etc.: Here, in this country, there is a solution for everything.

234. *bella ciudad de los paisajes:* the beautiful town of land-scapes.

235. *espléndido almuerzo:* splendid lunch; *habanos:* Havana cigars.

236. *cuartillas:* sheets of paper; *culto letrado:* a learned man of letters; *bellos parrafos:* fine sentences.

237. *culto y prestijioso letrado:* a learned and distinguished man of letters; *tan bello trabajo:* such a fine work.

238. *nutrida ovación:* an enthusiastic ovation.

244. *hacer daño*, etc.: she is going to make many victims through her beauty.

246–7. *El dia*, etc. . . . *vallados:* The day you were born, all the flowers blossomed . . . like the blackberries in the enclosures.

252. *mancornadores de novillitos:* amateur bull-fighters fighting against young bulls ; *Que bien torea*, etc. : How well this lad uses his *muleta!*

INDEX